BE WELL

MICRO-INTERVENTIONS FOR A MEANINGFUL LIFE

RAINA CHHAJER, PhD

notionpress.com

INDIA · SINGAPORE · MALAYSIA

ISBN
Hardcase 979-8-89610-685-2
Paperback 979-8-89610-299-1

Praise for
Be Well

"*Be Well* is a valuable resource for individuals seeking to enhance their well-being through evidence-based practices. Raina has crafted this wonderful book that integrates findings from positive psychology, nature connectedness, spirituality, and creative expression into simple yet impactful activities useful in fostering resilience, inner peace, and a deeper sense of fulfilment. With its holistic approach and practical tools, *Be Well* is a must-read for anyone looking to create lasting positive change and cultivating a more meaningful life."

Prof. Himanshu Rai, Director,
Indian Institute of Management Indore, India

"In times of growing fragmentation, chaos, violence, and uncertainty, the fundamental question of how we live our lives has become more crucial than ever. With remarkable insight and inspiration, Dr. Raina Chhajer delves into the enduring qualities that form the essence of our human experience – gratitude, kindness, flow, wholeness, arts, spirituality, nature, creativity, and more. She skilfully weaves together research and theory-based interventions, practices and reflections. This masterful integration makes the book an uplifting celebration that takes readers on a transformative, even therapeutic journey, offering guidance and practical wisdom in navigating the complexities of modern life. The book presents compelling ideas and engaging practical tools that will resonate with anyone seeking personal growth and a richer, more fulfilling life."

Prof. Pninit Russo-Netzer, Associate Professor,
Achva Academic College, Israel

"What you have in your hands with *Be Well* is a powerful guide to well-being, including practices from positive psychology, nature connection, spirituality, and creative expression. Raina acknowledges that well-being isn't one-size-fits-all, providing readers the flexibility to explore and adopt practices that resonate with their individual journeys and at their own pace. Cherish this book, apply its insights, and you'll find yourself on a transformative journey towards greater fulfilment and lasting happiness."

Dr. Ramya Ranganathan, Adjunct Faculty,
Indian Institute of Management Bangalore, India

"Be Well is an inspiring and practical guide for anyone seeking to cultivate greater balance, resilience, and joy in today's fast-paced world. Raina Chhajer seamlessly integrates evidence-based strategies with accessible tools for personal growth. Whether you're looking to reduce stress, deepen your connection to nature, or spark your creativity, this book is an invaluable companion for your well-being journey. Thoughtful, empowering, and deeply engaging, it's a roadmap to flourishing in every sense of the word."

Dr. Christopher Barnes, Senior Lecturer,
University of Derby, UK

Be Well is a gift to the soul, a guide for anyone seeking to nurture their inner self and live with higher purpose. This inspiring book invites readers to unlock their potential through practical tools and transformative practices, empowering them to show up for life with authenticity. No matter your starting point, *Be Well* helps you ignite your inner light.

Anup Gogate, Vice President,
APAC Sales at Neutrinos, Singapore

"Inspiring, practical, and transformative. *Be Well* bridges ancient wisdom with modern science, making it the perfect companion for anyone beginning their spiritual journey and seeking tools for mental health and well-being."

Virat Chirania, Director Programs,
Art of Living Foundation

To my sister *Neha*, for always believing
in me and standing by my side.

Table of Content

Section 3: Spirituality-Based Interventions
Introduction to spiritual practices
Concepts, theory, and research

Introduction

Welcome to a transformative journey through well-being, where science meets practice and theory blends with personal exploration. As an academic researcher, professor of psychology, certified forest therapy guide and yoga instructor, I am excited to share with you a synthesis of my experiences, insights, and passion for enhancing human flourishing. Along this journey, you will also find tools to help manage stress, alleviate feelings of anxiety, and combat loneliness, all of which are important for maintaining your mental health.

The pursuit of happiness has always been central to human life. Yet in today's fast-paced world, it's more crucial than ever to understand and consciously cultivate it, especially when dealing with stress or feelings of disconnection. Through my work, I've explored various pathways of well-being – positive psychology, the restorative power of nature, the profound impact of spiritual practices, and creative expression. This book reflects that journey, integrating these diverse fields into a cohesive framework designed to enhance your well-being and improve your mental health.

The structure of the book
This book is divided into four sections, each dedicated to a different aspect of well-being:

- **Positive-psychology interventions**: In this section, you'll explore foundational theories such as the PERMA model. You'll find practical activities designed to integrate these concepts into your life, helping you build resilience, reduce anxiety, foster meaningful relationships, and cultivate a sense of accomplishment, all of which contribute to your well-being.

- **Nature-based interventions**: Here, we'll examine the benefits of connecting with nature, drawing from theories like the biophilia hypothesis, stress reduction theory, and attention restoration theory. The activities in this section are designed to enhance your relationship with the natural world, improving well-being and physical health. These nature-based interventions are especially effective in reducing stress, promoting mental health, and alleviating feelings of loneliness.

- **Spirituality-based interventions**: Inspired by the teachings of Gurudev Sri Sri Ravi Shankar, this section explores spiritual practices such as yoga, pranayama, meditation, and service. These practices aim to help you connect with the sacred aspects of life, enhancing inner peace, self-awareness, and meaning in life. Spiritual tools can provide a refuge from daily stressors and reduce feelings of anxiety, helping you maintain a balanced and calm mental state.

- **Art-based interventions**: Creativity plays a vital role in well-being, explored through the lens of emotional regulation and flow. This section provides creative exercises designed to facilitate self-expression, emotional awareness, and stress reduction. Engaging in creative practices can help you process emotions, combat feelings of loneliness, and promote personal growth, leading to greater social connection and a lasting sense of accomplishment.

Is this book right for you?

As you begin this journey, you may wonder if this book will resonate with where you are in life. Let's explore if this is the right companion for your well-being journey:

- **Are you seeking more balance and fulfilment in your life?**
  If you're looking for practical ways to cultivate happiness, resilience, and a sense of purpose, this book provides evidence-based tools that can easily be integrated into your daily routine. Whether you're new to well-being practices or already on the path, you'll find activities that suit your needs and support your mental health.

- **Do you feel connected to nature or want to deepen that connection?**
  If you're drawn to the peace and serenity of the natural world but want to go beyond simply observing nature to truly connect with it, this book's section on nature connectedness will guide you through meaningful practices to enhance that bond. You'll learn how nature can be a powerful ally in reducing stress, increasing well-being, and combating feelings of disconnection.

- **Are you curious about spirituality and want to integrate a few practices into your life?**
  If you're looking for spiritual practices that foster inner peace and growth, the spirituality section introduces powerful techniques rooted in ancient wisdom to help you connect with the sacred in everyday life. These practices promote a deep sense of inner calm and self-awareness.

- **Do you thrive on creativity and self-expression?**
  If artistic or creative pursuits bring you joy, or if you want to explore how creativity can enhance your well-being, this book offers engaging exercises that promote self-expression, emotion regulation, and personal growth. You'll discover how creativity can unlock new perspectives and enhance emotional well-being.

Whether you're a professional seeking balance, a student managing stress, or someone yearning for a deeper sense of well-being, this book invites you to explore evidence-based practices in a holistic way. If you're ready to take a step toward a more fulfilling life, then yes – this book is for you.

How to begin this journey
Starting a well-being journey can feel exciting yet overwhelming. This book is designed to guide you every step of the way. Here's how you may begin:

- **Start where you are**: There's no need to rush or feel pressured to read the book in a specific order. Well-being is personal and your journey is unique. Begin with the section that resonates most with you – whether it's positive psychology, nature connectedness, spirituality, or creativity – and allow yourself the freedom to explore what feels right in the moment.
- **Set an intention**: Take a moment to reflect on what you hope to achieve from this journey. Is it a deeper connection with yourself? More inner peace? Greater creativity or engagement with life? Setting an intention provides focus as you move through the book.
- **Engage fully with the activities**: The heart of this book lies not just in understanding the theories but in actively engaging with the practices. Pick a few activities that speak to you and try them with an open mind. These exercises are designed to be accessible and flexible, allowing you to tailor them to your own schedule and lifestyle – whether you have five minutes or an entire afternoon.
- **Pace yourself**: Well-being is a lifelong journey, not a race. There's no need to rush through the sections or activities. Take your time to reflect, adapt, and make the

practices your own. What matters most is consistency and maintaining a sense of curiosity and openness as you explore each new idea.

- **Be gentle with yourself**: Like any personal growth journey, there may be ups and downs. You might find some practices easy and others more challenging, and that's fine. Approach each experience with kindness, recognizing that growth takes time.
- **Track your progress**: Journaling or reflecting on your experiences can provide valuable insights. Tracking your progress will not only help you stay motivated but also give you a deeper understanding of what practices resonate most with you.

I invite you to embark on this journey with me, exploring different well-being interventions. Together, we'll discover new ways to enhance our happiness, find meaning in life, and embrace the beauty of human flourishing. Enjoy the journey!

Section I

Positive Psychology Interventions

Science of well-being

The pursuit of happiness has been a fundamental aspect of human existence for centuries. As our understanding of what constitutes a fulfilling and flourishing life has evolved, so too have the methods by which we seek to achieve it. Positive psychology, an evolving field within psychology, provides theoretical underpinning to understand and enhance the quality of our life. One of the most comprehensive theoretical framework in this domain is the PERMA model of well-being, which serves as the base for the micro interventions and insights presented in this section.

Understanding the PERMA Model

The PERMA model, developed by psychologist Martin Seligman, is a framework that identifies five core elements essential for well-being. These elements are positive emotion, engagement, relationships, meaning, and accomplishment. According to Seligman, these five elements are integral to human flourishing and can significantly enhance our overall quality of life.

- **Positive emotion** refers to the experience of joy, gratitude, and other uplifting feelings that contribute to a sense of happiness and satisfaction. Cultivating positive emotions helps us build resilience and better cope with life's challenges.
- **Engagement** is about being deeply involved in activities that absorb and captivate us. When we are fully engaged, we experience a state of flow, where our skills and challenges are perfectly aligned, leading to a sense of fulfilment and joy.

- **Relationships** emphasize the importance of forming and maintaining meaningful connections with others. Positive, supportive relationships are a key predictor of well-being and can provide a sense of belonging and purpose.
- **Meaning** involves having a sense of purpose and feeling that our lives are part of something greater than ourselves. Engaging in activities that align with our values and contribute to the well-being of others enhances our sense of meaning.
- **Accomplishment** reflects the pursuit and attainment of goals. Achieving personal and professional milestones provides a sense of achievement and boosts our self-esteem and motivation.

The importance of the science of well-being

Understanding the science of well-being is crucial for human flourishing. It equips us with the knowledge and tools to enhance our own lives and support others in their journeys toward greater fulfilment. By applying principles from the PERMA model, we can engage in activities that build these five elements, leading to a more enriched and meaningful life.

This section of the book delves into various activities that embody the core concepts of the PERMA model. Each activity is crafted to help individuals explore and integrate these elements into their daily lives. For example, activities like writing a gratitude letter or savouring old memories are designed to enhance positive emotions. Interventions like active listening and engaging in personal project focus on relationships and engagement. Similarly, exercises such as setting goals or crafting a personal growth timeline focus on accomplishment and meaning.

By engaging with these micro interventions, readers will have the opportunity to experience the benefits of applying the science of well-being. Whether it's through practicing self-compassion, exploring strengths, or embracing a growth mindset, these activities offer practical and actionable ways to improve overall well-being.

In essence, this section on positive psychology interventions provides a roadmap for living a more fulfilling and flourishing life. It offers valuable insights into how we can cultivate happiness, build resilience, and achieve our fullest potential. As you journey through this section and engage with the activities, remember that the pursuit of well-being is not a destination but a continuous process of growth and self-discovery. By embracing the principles of the PERMA model, you are taking meaningful steps towards a richer and more satisfying life.

Gratitude letter writing: Words from the heart

Gratitude is the intentional recognition of life's positive aspects, helping shift our focus from what's lacking to what's present; research indicates that practicing gratitude enhances well-being, reducing symptoms of depression and anxiety while promoting resilience and life satisfaction. Scientific studies show that gratitude activates brain regions linked to emotional regulation, fostering positive emotions and reducing stress.

Time: 10–15 minutes

Location: A quiet indoor or outdoor space

You will need:

- Pen and paper

You will learn:

- How to be fully present while expressing gratitude.
- How to cultivate a sense of appreciation for someone important in your life.

Before you begin:

- **Choose your person:** Think of someone who has made a positive impact in your life. This could be a friend, family member, mentor, or anyone who has offered support, kindness, or love.
- **Breathe and relax:** Sit comfortably, take a few deep breaths, and clear your mind of distractions. Let go of any tension, focusing on feelings of warmth and appreciation for this person.

Activity instructions:

- **Prepare to connect:** Close your eyes and visualise the person you are writing to. Think about specific moments when they helped or supported you. Take a few deep breaths, centring yourself in these memories of gratitude.

- **Write your letter:** Begin your letter addressing the person with "Dear [Name]..." Express why you are grateful. Mention specific moments or qualities you appreciate. Focus on how their presence has impacted your life positively, whether through small acts or major support.
- **Tune into your feelings:** As you write, be aware of your emotions. Notice if any warmth, joy, or even tears arise. Let the process of writing bring out the depth of your appreciation.
- **Stay present:** Spend the next few minutes writing freely. Let the words flow without overthinking. Simply focus on your breath and the heartfelt message you're conveying.
- **End with gratitude:** When you've finished, conclude the letter by thanking the person for being part of your life. Take a final deep breath, holding onto the feeling of gratitude.

Alternative activities:
- **Letter delivery:** If possible, consider delivering the letter in person or sending it by email. The act of sharing your gratitude can further strengthen your relationship.
- **Gratitude journal:** Each day, write three things you're grateful for, focusing on the positive feelings and meaningful experiences they evoke.

Reflection:
- How did it feel to express your gratitude in writing?
- What emotions surfaced during the process?
- Did this activity deepen your appreciation for the person you wrote to?

Savouring an old memory:
Revisiting joyful moments

Savouring is the intentional practice of fully immersing oneself in positive experiences, enhancing enjoyment, and appreciation of joyful moments. This practice significantly boosts well-being by increasing happiness, reducing anxiety and depression. The broaden-and-build theory explains that savouring fosters positive emotions that broadens cognitive processes and over time build resources, that further enhance resilience and life satisfaction. Research shows that savouring positive memories can create a buffer against negative emotions and distress, helping individuals cope more effectively with adverse situations, thus promoting long-term mental health and emotional resources.

Time: 10–15 minutes
Location: A quiet indoor or outdoor space
You will need:
- A comfortable place to sit
- A journal or notebook (optional)
- An artefact related to the memory (e.g., a photo)

You will learn:
- How to recognise and amplify positive emotions.
- How to cultivate the ability to stay present with a memory and savour its impact.
- How to strengthen your sense of happiness by focusing on uplifting past experiences.

Before you begin:
- **Choose a memory:** Think of a joyful or meaningful memory – an experience that brought you happiness,

peace, or excitement. It could be something simple, like a day spent with loved ones or a significant milestone in your life.

- **Prepare your artefact:** Select an object related to this memory, such as a photograph from the event, a souvenir, or memorabilia.
- **Relax and get comfortable:** Sit in a quiet place where you will be undisturbed. Close your eyes and take a few deep breaths, allowing your body and mind to relax.

Activity Instructions:
- **Recall the memory:** With your eyes closed, bring the chosen memory into your mind. Picture it vividly, recalling the sights, sounds, and people involved. Focus on the details that made the experience special.
- **Savour the emotions:** As the memory becomes clearer, pay attention to the emotions it evokes. Are you feeling joy, warmth, love, or excitement? Allow yourself to bask in these positive feelings and let them fill you.
- **Engage with the artefact:** Open your eyes and gently interact with your artefact. If it is a photo, look closely at the image and let the details trigger the memory. Hold it if it is a momento, and let its presence remind you of the experience. Notice how the artefact helps deepen your connection to the memory.
- **Tune into your senses:** Notice how your body feels. Can you remember the sounds, smells, or textures from that time? Let your senses enhance the vividness of the memory.
- **Stay with the moment:** Let your mind stay with the memory for the next few minutes, replaying it as if you're reliving it. Resist the urge to rush through it –

simply allow the feelings of joy and contentment to linger.

- **Reflect on its impact:** Think about why this memory stands out. How did it shape you? What lasting emotions or lessons did it leave behind? Acknowledge the positive impact it has on your current well-being.
- **Express gratitude:** Before concluding, take a moment to feel grateful for the experience. Silently thank yourself and the people involved for the joy this memory continues to bring.

Alternative activities:
- **Savouring a meal:** Take time to fully enjoy your favourite meal. Notice the flavours, textures, and aromas with each bite. Pause between bites and reflect on the pleasure it brings.
- **Moment-capturing journal:** Write about special moments in your day. Describe the details that made the experience enjoyable, including your feelings, sensations, and thoughts to relive and savour later.

Reflection:
- How did it feel to relive the memory?
- What emotions surfaced as you focused on the experience?
- Did this activity enhance your appreciation of the past and its impact on your mood?

Kindness ripples: Everyday acts of impact

Random acts of kindness are spontaneous gestures aimed at improving the well-being of others, fostering a sense of community and connection. Engaging in these acts not only enhances the lives of those on the receiving end but also significantly benefits the mental health of those who perform them. Research has shown that practicing kindness can lead to increased happiness, reduced stress, and lower levels of depression. The longest study on happiness, conducted by Harvard University, found that strong social connections and altruistic behaviours are key factors in long-term emotional well-being, highlighting the profound impact of kindness on our overall happiness and mental health.

Time: 30–60 minutes
Location: Anywhere you can interact with others (e.g., home, office, community space)
You will need:
- A notebook or journal
- Pens or markers
- Small cards or notes (optional)

You will learn:
- The impact of kindness on others and yourself.
- How small, thoughtful actions can create positive ripples in your community.
- Techniques for incorporating kindness into your daily routine.

Activity instructions:
- **Set up your kindness space:** Choose a quiet, comfortable space where you can focus on planning

and executing your acts of kindness. Gather your notebook or journal and any small cards or notes you might use for your acts of kindness.

- **Brainstorm random acts of kindness:** Spend a few minutes brainstorming a list of simple, thoughtful acts of kindness you can perform. Examples include:
  - Complimenting a colleague or friend.
  - Paying for someone's tea or meal.
  - Sending a heartfelt note or message.
  - Offering to help with a task.
  - Sharing positive feedback with someone.
  - Holding the door open for someone.
  - Sending a text of appreciation.
  - Offering a smile.
- **Choose your acts:** Choose 2–3 acts of kindness from your list that you can perform during the activity session. Aim for a mix of different types of acts, depending on what feels most meaningful to you.
- **Perform the acts:** Execute each selected act of kindness. Pay attention to how it feels to give and how the recipient responds. If you're giving a card or note, you might include a brief, uplifting message.
- **Journal your thoughts:** After completing your acts of kindness, write down your reflections in your notebook or journal. Consider the following prompts:
  - How did it feel to perform these acts?
  - What was the reaction of the people you helped?
  - Did you notice any changes in your own mood or perspective?
- **Plan to continue:** Think about how you can integrate random acts of kindness into your daily life. Set a goal to perform one act of kindness each week or each day and keep track of your progress.

Alternative activities:

- **Kindness challenge:** Organize a kindness challenge with friends or family. Each person performs a random act of kindness and shares their experience with the group.
- **Notes for strangers:** Write anonymous notes of encouragement or appreciation and leave them in public places for others to find, such as on a bulletin board or in a library book.

Reflection:

- How did performing random acts of kindness affect your mood and outlook?
- What did you learn about the impact of kindness on others?
- How can you continue to incorporate kindness into your daily routine?

Strength spotting: Discover, develop, and deploy

Character strengths are positive traits and qualities that contribute to an individual's overall well-being. Identifying and cultivating these strengths, such as gratitude, social intellegence, or perseverance, fosters personal growth, resilience, and enhanced relationships. Research indicates that focusing on strengths is linked to improved mental health outcomes, such as decreased anxiety and depression, and increased life satisfaction. Leveraging our strengths fosters a sense of purpose and agency, helping us navigate challenges more effectively. By actively engaging with our unique abilities, we not only enhance our own well-being but also contribute positively to the lives of those around us.

Time: 30–45 minutes
Location: A quiet and comfortable space
You will need:
- A notebook or journal
- Pens or markers
- A computer to take the VIA character strengths survey

You will learn:
- How to identify and recognise your unique strengths and VIA character strengths.
- Techniques for reflecting on and celebrating your abilities and traits.
- Strategies for applying these strengths in various aspects of your life.

Activity instructions:
- **Introduction to strength**: Recognise your strengths, including VIA character strengths, and how they contribute to personal growth and fulfilment.

- **Take the VIA survey:** If you haven't taken the VIA character strengths survey, complete it online at VIA survey of character strengths. This survey will provide a detailed profile of your top strengths. Examine your five top character strengths and how they align with your experiences.
- **Other strength identification:** Also, reflect on other personal strengths you've identified through past experiences. Write down your top strengths and note specific examples or achievements where these strengths were evident.
- **Seek feedback:** Ask a friend or family member to provide feedback on the strengths they see in you. Share your VIA character strengths and personal examples with them if you like. Compare their feedback with your self-assessment. Discuss any new insights or validations they provide.
- **Celebrate your strengths:** Acknowledge and celebrate your identified strengths. Reflect on how these strengths have contributed to your successes and personal growth.
- **Action plan:** Develop specific actions or goals that leverage your top strengths in different areas of your life, such as career, relationships, or personal development.

Alternative activities:
- **Strengths storytelling:** Write a story about yourself as a superhero, with your strengths as your "superpowers." Describe a scenario where you use these powers to overcome obstacles or help others.
- **Strengths in action reflection:** Choose a challenge or goal you're working on and reflect on which strengths

you can apply to the situation. Write about how you can use those strengths to approach the challenge differently and how they might help you succeed.

Reflection:
- How did identifying and celebrating your strengths enhance your self-awareness and confidence?
- What new insights did you gain from feedback and personal reflection?
- How can you apply your strengths to improve various aspects of your life? What changes or benefits do you expect?

Please scan the QR code for the link to
VIA strengths survey.

Deep celebration: Micro wins to overcome negativity bias

Negativity bias is the brain's innate tendency to focus on and recall negative experiences more than positive ones, a survival mechanism that can lead to persistent feelings of anxiety and dissatisfaction. Actively cultivating positive emotions can counter this bias, enhance resilience, improve mental health, and promote well-being. Research indicates that recognizing and celebrating micro wins – small achievements in daily life – significantly boosts mood and fosters a sense of accomplishment. This practice activates the brain's reward system, releasing neurotransmitters like dopamine, which enhance feelings of happiness and satisfaction. By training ourselves to acknowledge and savour these positive moments, we can create a buffer against negativity, leading to greater emotional resilience and a more balanced perspective on life.

Time: 30–45 minutes
Location: A comfortable and inspiring space
You will need:
- A notebook or journal
- Pens or markers
- Small reward items or tokens (e.g., stickers, treats, or any small item that feels rewarding)
- A list of recent achievements or positive moments

You will learn:
- How to recognize and celebrate small achievements to boost motivation and well-being.
- Techniques to counteract negativity bias by focusing on positive accomplishments.

- The role of small rewards in enhancing positive emotions and reinforcing progress.

Activity instructions:
- **Set the stage:** Find a comfortable, inspiring area where you can reflect and celebrate without interruptions. Have your notebook or journal, small reward items, and any recent achievement lists ready.
- **Identify your micro wins:** Take a moment to list recent accomplishments, no matter how small. These could be completed tasks, positive interactions, or personal improvements.
- **Celebrate micro wins:** Write each achievement in your notebook. Note how these small wins contribute to your overall goals and well-being. For each micro win, jot down a few positive aspects or benefits of the achievement. Reflect on how it made you feel and why it's significant.
- **Reward yourself:** Select a small reward that feels meaningful to you. This could be a treat, a sticker, or any item that symbolizes celebration. Use the reward to acknowledge and reinforce the positive feelings associated with your achievements.
- **Journal your thoughts:** Write down how celebrating your micro wins and using rewards impacted your mood and outlook. Consider the following prompts:
    - How did focusing on micro wins affect your perception of recent achievements?
    - Did the rewards enhance your positive emotions?
    - How did this activity help counteract any negativity bias?

Alternative activities:
- **Celebration jar:** Create a jar where you add notes about micro wins or positive experiences throughout the week. Review them weekly to acknowledge your achievements and counter negativity.
- **Micro win celebration ritual:** Develop a personal ritual for celebrating micro wins, such as lighting a candle, playing your favourite song, or treating yourself to something enjoyable whenever you achieve a small goal.

Reflection:
- How did acknowledging and celebrating micro wins affect your mood and motivation?
- How did the use of small rewards enhance your positive feelings and reinforce progress?
- How did focusing on positive achievements help combat any existing negativity bias?

Active listening: Being present in a conversation

Active listening involves fully engaging with the speaker to understand their message and respond thoughtfully, fostering deeper connections and trust in both personal and professional relationships. This practice enhances well-being by promoting empathy, reducing stress, and increasing emotional intelligence, which is crucial for maintaining healthy interactions. Scientific research shows that active listening activates neural pathways related to empathy and emotional regulation, improving communication skills and contributing to greater satisfaction and a sense of belonging in relationships.

Time: 20–30 minutes
Location: Home, workplace, or any social setting
You will need:
- A notebook or journal
- A timer or clock

You will learn:
- How to stay fully present and engaged during conversations.
- Techniques for deep listening to understand and connect with others more effectively.
- Strategies for enhancing empathy and comprehension in your interactions.

Activity instructions:
- **Preparation for presence:** Identify a topic you are interested in or a recent conversation you'd like to revisit. This could be something meaningful or a topic you wish to discuss with a friend.

- **Deep listening exercise:** Allocate 10–15 minutes for the exercise. Involve a friend or family member to have a conversation with you on the chosen topic.
- **Active listening:** Practice focusing entirely on the speaker. Pay close attention to their words, tone, and body language. Allow the speaker to finish their thoughts completely before responding. Resist the urge to formulate your reply while they are speaking.
- **Reflect and paraphrase:** After the speaker finishes, reflect on what was said and paraphrase their main points. For example, "So, what I hear you saying is..." This helps ensure you've understood their message correctly.
- **Reflect on the experience:** After the conversation, take a few minutes to reflect on the following questions:
    - How did it feel to be fully present during the conversation?
    - What challenges did you encounter in staying focused and listening deeply?
    - How did reflecting and paraphrasing impact your understanding of the speaker's message?
    - Did you notice any changes in how you connected with the speaker or in your own emotional responses?
- **Plan for future practice:** Identify specific strategies you can use to practice being present and listening deeply in future conversations. For example, you might decide to:
    - Practice deep breathing before conversations to improve focus.
    - Set a goal to actively listen in your next interactions.
    - Work on managing distractions during conversations.

Alternative activities:
- **Presence reminders:** Create visual or digital reminders to prompt you to practice being present during conversations. For example, use a sticky note or phone reminder with a prompt like "Be here now!" to remind you of your goal.
- **Listening buddy:** Partner with a friend or colleague to regularly practice deep listening with each other. Provide feedback and support to enhance each other's listening skills.

Reflection:
- How did focusing on being present affect your experience of the conversation?
- What improvements did you notice in your understanding of the speaker's message and your connection with them?
- How can you integrate deep listening techniques into your everyday conversations to enhance communication and empathy?

Dear future me: A letter to your best self

Optimism is the mindset of expecting positive outcomes and viewing challenges as opportunities for growth, which enhances resilience, motivation, and overall well-being. Scientific research shows that cultivating optimism activates neural pathways linked to hope and positive emotions, enabling better coping skills and emotional regulation. Practices like the best self exercise, where individuals visualize their strengths and aspirations, further reinforce this optimistic mindset, improving emotional intelligence and fostering stronger relationships, ultimately supporting mental health and thriving.

Time: 30–45 minutes
Location: A quiet and comfortable space
You will need:
- A notebook or journal
- Pens or markers
- An envelope (optional)

You will learn:
- How to articulate your aspirations and values in a meaningful way.
- Techniques for reflecting on your personal growth and future goals.
- Strategies for using written reflection as a tool for motivation and self-improvement.

Activity instructions:
- **Set up your space:** Find a quiet, comfortable place where you can write without distractions. Gather your notebook or journal and pens. If you're using an envelope and stamp, have those ready too.

- **Reflect on your best self:** Consider the qualities, achievements, and behaviours you associate with your best self. Reflect on what makes you proud and what you hope to achieve.
- **Visualize your ideal future:** Imagine yourself a few years from now, having achieved your goals and living in alignment with your values. Think about how you feel, what you've accomplished, and how you've grown.
- **Write the letter:** Begin the letter with a warm greeting to yourself, such as "Dear [Your Name]," or "Dear Best Self." Write about your dreams, goals, and the qualities you admire in your best self. Describe what your ideal future looks like and how you plan to get there. Include words of encouragement and support for any challenges you may face. Acknowledge your strengths and remind yourself of your ability to overcome obstacles. Thank yourself for the efforts you're making towards personal growth and for being committed to living your best life.
- **Identify specific areas:** Note specific areas where you want to grow, such as improving communication skills, building confidence, or developing new hobbies. Identify aspects of your health and wellness that you'd like to focus on, like creating a balanced diet, establishing a regular exercise routine, or practicing mindfulness. Outline career aspirations or goals you wish to achieve, such as advancing in your profession, pursuing further education, or starting a personal project.
- **Store for future reading:** Place the letter in an envelope if you have one. Keep the letter in a safe place where you can read it in the future. You might choose to open

it on a specific date, such as a milestone anniversary or a time when you need motivation.

- **Set action steps:** After writing, take a moment to review what you've written. Reflect on how it feels to articulate your aspirations and self-encouragement. Based on your letter, identify one or two actionable steps you can take to move closer to your best self.

Alternative activities:
- **Follow-up letter:** Write a follow-up letter to your future self, imagining how you'll reflect on your achievements and growth. Set a date to open and read it later.
- **Gratitude to self:** Write a separate letter expressing gratitude to yourself for specific accomplishments or qualities. This can reinforce positive self-regard and motivation.

Reflection:
- How did writing the letter to your best self-affect your motivation and outlook on your goals?
- What did you learn about your aspirations and values through this exercise?
- How can you use the insights from your letter to guide your actions and decisions moving forward?

Self-compassion breaks: Being kind to yourself

Self-compassion is the practice of treating yourself with the same kindness, understanding, and care that you would offer a friend, and it encompasses three key dimensions: self-kindness, which involves caring for oneself during challenging times; common humanity, acknowledging that suffering is a universal experience; and mindfulness, which entails recognizing negative emotions without over-identifying with them. This practice fosters emotional resilience and enhances overall well-being by promoting adaptive coping strategies, such as problem-solving and seeking social support, emphasizing its role in nurturing a balanced mindset that mitigates stress and supports mental health.

Time: 5–10 minutes per break
Location: Any location where you can have a brief moment of quiet
You will need:
- A quiet space (even a small area will work)
- A notebook or journal (optional)
- A timer or alarm (optional)

You will learn:
- How to take quick breaks to practice self-compassion throughout your day.
- Strategies for incorporating self-compassion breaks into your daily routine.

Activity instructions:
- **Find your spot:** Identify a quiet space where you can take a short break. This could be a corner of your home, a quiet room at work, or even a peaceful outdoor spot.

- **Initiate the break:** Take a deep breath and pause whatever you are doing. Allow yourself a moment of calm and presence. Recognize any stress, frustration, or self-criticism you may be experiencing. Briefly identify what you are feeling and why.
- **Practice self-compassion:** Use a kind and supportive statement to address yourself. For example: "It's okay to feel overwhelmed. I'm doing my best, and that's enough." Close your eyes if you're comfortable and focus on your breath. Reflect on how you can treat yourself with kindness and understanding in this moment.
- **Engage in soothing action:** Choose a simple activity that brings you comfort. This could be stretching, taking a few deep breaths, or even gently placing a hand on your heart. Imagine a peaceful, supportive scene or memory that helps you feel calm and centered.
- **Resume mindfully:** Return to your activities with a refreshed mindset and a sense of self-compassion.

Alternative activities:
- **Scheduled breaks:** Set reminders throughout your day to take self-compassion breaks. Use a timer or an app to prompt you to pause and practice kindness.
- **Compassion cards:** Create small cards with self-compassionate statements or affirmations. Keep them handy to read during your breaks.

Reflection:
- How did taking a self-compassion break affect your stress levels and emotional state?

- What did you learn about your own needs for self-compassion during these breaks?
- How can you continue to incorporate self-compassion breaks into your daily routine for ongoing support and well-being?

Experience flow: Immersive personal project exploration

Flow is a state of deep focus and immersion that occurs when an individual's skills are optimally matched to the challenges presented by an activity, leading to a complete engagement that makes time feel irrelevant. This experience significantly enhances well-being by promoting positive emotions, fostering peak performance, and encouraging a sense of fulfilment, while also reducing stress and anxiety. The science behind flow highlights that achieving this balance between skill and challenge not only leads to higher engagement levels but also boosts intrinsic motivation and overall life satisfaction.

Time: 30–60 minutes
Location: A quiet, comfortable indoor space
You will need:
- A comfortable place to work.
- Materials related to your personal project (e.g., documents, tools, art supplies)
- A notebook or journal

You will learn:
- How to achieve a flow state by deeply engaging in a personal project.
- Techniques to enhance focus and immersion in your work.
- Insights into how personal projects can facilitate a flow experience.

Before you begin:
- **Select your project:** Choose a personal project that excites and interests you. It could be anything from writing a story, developing a business plan, creating

art, working on a DIY project, or learning a new skill. Ensure you are passionate about it and willing to invest time in it.

- **Prepare your workspace:** Set up a quiet, comfortable space to focus without interruptions. Gather all the materials and resources you'll need for your project.
- **Set an intention:** Reflect on your goals for this session. Decide what specific aspect of the project you want to work on and what you hope to achieve during the time you have.

Activity instructions:
- **Begin working:** Start working on your project. Focus on the task at hand and let yourself get absorbed in the details. Avoid distractions and try to stay fully engaged with the work.
- **Embrace the challenge:** Approach any difficulties or challenges as part of the creative process. Use them as opportunities to experiment and problem-solve, enhancing your immersion and engagement.
- **Monitor your experience:** Pay attention to how you feel as you work. Notice if you are losing track of time, feeling deeply concentrated, or experiencing a sense of effortless involvement in your work. These are signs that you might be experiencing a flow state.
- **Adjust as needed:** If you find yourself getting distracted or frustrated, take a short break, reassess your goals, and then return to the project with a fresh perspective. Adjust your approach to maintain focus and engagement.
- **Reflect on flow:** When you are done, take a moment to reflect on your experience. Did you experience a sense

of deep immersion or timelessness? What aspects of the project or your approach helped you achieve flow?
- **Document your experience:** Write down your reflections in your journal. Note any insights about how you experienced flow and what factors contributed to it. Consider how you might replicate these conditions in future sessions.

Alternative activities:
- **Coding or problem-solving:** Work on solving a complex coding challenge or puzzle. Stay fully engaged in finding solutions, enjoying the satisfaction of each small breakthrough.
- **Playing a musical instrument:** Practice a musical piece that challenges you but is within your skill level. Concentrate on the rhythm and melody, letting the music guide your focus.

Reflection:
- How did engaging in your personal project affect your experience of flow?
- What specific project or work process elements contributed to a sense of immersion?
- Did you notice any changes in your mood or productivity due to focusing deeply on the project?

Energy snapshot: Enhancing your daily vitality

Energy management is the practice of balancing physical, mental, emotional, and spiritual energy to enhance productivity and well-being. This approach fosters resilience, mitigates burnout, and improves mental health by encouraging individuals to prioritize rest, set boundaries, and cultivate self-awareness. Research supports that optimizing energy levels rather than merely managing time leads to better focus and engagement. Studies indicate that regular breaks and restorative practices can replenish energy reserves, enhancing cognitive function and emotional regulation. Additionally, maintaining a balance among different types of energy promotes sustainable productivity, allowing individuals to perform optimally over time.

Time: 30–45 minutes
Location: Anywhere with the ability to record observations (e.g., home, office, outdoor space)
You will need:
- A notebook or journal
- Pens or markers
- A smartphone or smartwatch with a note-taking app (optional)
- Tools for enhancing energy

You will learn:
- How to track and understand fluctuations in your energy levels throughout the day.
- Techniques for enhancing physical, emotional, mental, and spiritual energy.
- Insights into how daily routines and activities impact overall energy.

Activity instructions:

- **Set up your energy tracking:** Prepare your notebook or journal for recording your observations. You can also use a note-taking app on your smartphone or smartwatch. Draw a simple chart or table with columns for time, energy levels and what task you might be doing at that moment.
- **Track your energy levels:** Throughout the day, at regular intervals (every 1-2 hours), note your energy levels. Use a scale from 1 to 10, where 1 is very low energy and 10 is very high energy. Pay attention to how your energy levels change in response to different activities, meals, interactions, or periods of rest.
- **Analyse your chart:** Look over your recorded data and identify any noticeable patterns or trends. For example, do you experience a slump in energy after lunch or a boost during exercising? Write down any observations in your journal. Consider how different times of day or activities or interactions impact your energy levels.
- **Enhance your energy:** Select one tool for each energy category and apply it:
    - **Physical energy:** Engage in a quick workout or stretch to boost your physical energy.
    - **Mental energy:** Unplug from screens and technology for a dedicated time period to refresh your mind.
    - **Emotional energy:** Take a moment to practice understanding or empathy towards someone else, which can enhance emotional energy.
    - **Spiritual energy:** Engage in a brief meditation practice to connect with your inner self and boost spiritual energy.

- **Implement the tool:** Use the chosen tool for each energy category and observe its immediate effects on your energy levels. Record your experience and any changes in your energy levels in your journal. Reflect on how each tool impacted your physical, emotional, mental, or spiritual energy.

Alternative activities:
- **Energy audit:** Conduct a weekly audit of your daily routines. List activities and rate them on a scale of 1-10 for energy impact. Focus on incorporating more high-energy activities into your schedule.
- **Energy boost challenges:** Design weekly challenges to enhance your energy levels, such as drinking more water, trying a new exercise, or practicing gratitude daily. Reflect on the impact of these changes on your vitality.

Reflection:
- How did tracking your energy levels help you understand your daily fluctuations?
- How did each selected tool affect your energy in its respective category?
- How can you use your observations and the tools to improve your overall energy management throughout the day?

Growth mindset: Reward the process and embrace 'not yet'

A growth mindset is the belief that abilities and intelligence can be developed through dedication, effort, and learning. By embracing challenges and viewing setbacks as opportunities for growth, this mindset fosters resilience, reduces anxiety, and encourages persistence. The science behind this mindset is rooted in neuroplasticity, which indicates that engaging in challenging tasks and persisting through difficulties can result in physical changes in the brain, enhancing learning and adaptability. Research shows that those with a growth mindset are more likely to employ adaptive coping strategies and exhibit better emotional regulation, leading to greater success and life satisfaction.

Time: 45–60 minutes
Location: A quiet and comfortable space
You will need:
- A notebook or journal
- Pens or markers
- Sticky notes
- Small rewards (e.g., a treat, a small gift, or a break)

You will learn:
- How to adopt a growth mindset by focusing on the concept of "not yet."
- Techniques to reframe challenges as opportunities for learning and growth.
- Strategies for rewarding progress to reinforce motivation and celebrate achievements.

Activity instructions:

- **Understanding growth mindset:** Briefly review the idea of a growth mindset and the concept of "not yet"" i.e. believing that abilities can be developed through effort and learning. Now think about areas in your life where you may have a fixed mindset. Reflect on how adopting a growth mindset could change your approach to these areas.

- **Identify fixed mindset:** Write down 2-3 areas where you feel challenged or where progress seems slow. These could be related to personal goals, work tasks, or new skills. Note any fixed mindset thoughts you have about these challenges, such as "I'm not good at this" or "This will never change."

- **Reframe with "not yet":** For each challenge, reframe your fixed mindset thoughts into growth mindset statements by adding "not yet." For example, change "I'm not good at this" to "I'm not good at this yet." Use sticky notes to write these reframed beliefs. Place them somewhere visible to remind yourself of your growth mindset.

- **Reward each step:** For each challenge, list actionable steps you can take to move forward. Focus on the process of learning and effort rather than immediate outcomes. Decide on a small reward for each step you complete. It could be something like enjoying a favourite treat, taking a break, or indulging in a small gift. Write down these rewards in your journal.

- **Track progress:** As you work on your action plan, mark off completed steps and reward yourself accordingly. Reflect on how rewarding yourself enhances motivation and reinforces your growth mindset.

- **Continued growth:** Reflect on how reframing your mindset and rewarding progress affected your motivation and feelings. How did adopting a growth mindset change your approach to the challenges? What impact did the rewards have on your motivation and perception of progress?

Alternative activities:
- **Reward the process:** Create a board where you write down goals or skills you haven't mastered yet. For each one, write down small steps you're taking toward achieving it, focusing on the progress rather than the endpoint.
- **Reflection time:** Dedicate 10 minutes each day to reflect on one area where you're applying effort but haven't achieved mastery yet. Ask yourself: "What did I learn today?" and "How can I improve tomorrow?"

Reflection:
- How did the process of reframing challenges as "not yet" affect your approach and mindset?
- How did the rewards influence your motivation and progress?
- How can you use the strategies from this activity to continue fostering a growth mindset and rewarding progress in other areas of your life?

Being resilient: Knowing your sources

Resilience is the ability to bounce back from adversity, challenges, and setbacks with strength and adaptability. This quality enhances a positive outlook, encouraging learning from difficulties, and fostering perseverance, ultimately leading to reduced stress and anxiety. The science behind resilience indicates that it involves both psychological and biological processes. Studies have shown that resilient individuals often exhibit greater emotional regulation and problem-solving abilities, which are associated with the brain's capacity to adapt and form new connections. Research also highlights the role of social support, as positive relationships can buffer against stress and foster resilience.

Time: 45–60 minutes
Location: A quiet, comfortable indoor space
You will need:
- A notebook or journal
- Pens or markers
- Sticky notes
- A comfortable place to sit

You will learn:
- How to identify and reflect on the sources of your resilience.
- Techniques for understanding how these sources have supported you through challenges.
- Insights into leveraging your sources of resilience for future challenges.

Activity instructions:

- **Prepare your space:** Find a quiet, comfortable space where you can focus and reflect without interruptions. Have your notebook or journal, pens or markers, and sticky notes ready.
- **Identify past challenges:** In your notebook or journal, list some significant challenges or difficult situations you have faced in the past. For each challenge, jot down what helped you get through it. This could include internal qualities (like determination or optimism) or external supports (such as friends, family, or resources).
- **Sources of resilience:** On separate sticky notes, write down specific sources of your resilience you identified. For example, you might have "family support," "personal strengths," "past successes," or "community resources." Arrange these notes in your notebook or on a flat surface in categories or clusters to visualize their roles.
- **Deep dive reflection:** For each source of resilience, write a detailed reflection in your journal.
  - What is this source of resilience? Describe it in detail.
  - How has it helped you in the past? Include specific examples or situations.
  - Why is this source important to you? Explore its significance and impact.
  - How can you continue to use or strengthen this source? Think about ways to keep this source active or leverage it more effectively.
- **Create a resilience plan:** Reflect on how you can apply these sources of resilience to upcoming or potential future challenges. Write down action steps or strategies for utilizing these sources effectively. Develop a plan

or a personal mantra based on your reflections. This can serve as a guide to remind you of your strengths when facing new challenges.

Alternative activities:
- **Resilience playlist:** Compile a playlist of songs that inspire you or remind you of your strength during tough times. Listen to it when you need a boost, reflecting on how the music resonates with your resilience journey.
- **Resilience web:** Create a web diagram with "Resilience" at the centre. Around it, add branches representing sources of strength – such as family, friends, values, skills, and personal beliefs – and reflect on how each supported you during tough times.

Reflection:
- How did identifying your sources of resilience help you understand your strength?
- What did you learn about yourself through this reflective process?
- How will you use these insights to handle future challenges or build further resilience?

Goal quest: Setting your learning and performance goals

Goal setting involves defining clear objectives to achieve desired outcomes, enhancing direction and motivation. Learning goals focus on skill acquisition and personal growth, while performance goals target specific achievements. Both types positively impact well-being; learning goals foster resilience and a love for learning, whereas performance goals boost motivation and self-esteem. Research shows that learning goals promote intrinsic motivation, leading to deeper engagement, while performance goals can increase focus but may induce anxiety if overly pressured. A balanced approach integrating both types is recommended for optimal outcomes.

Time: 45–60 minutes
Location: A quiet and comfortable space
You will need:
- A notebook or journal
- Pens or markers
- Sticky notes or index cards
- A large piece of paper or poster board (optional)
- Coloured pens or markers (optional)

You will learn:
- The difference between learning and performance goals and their significance.
- How to set clear, actionable milestones for achieving your goals.
- Techniques for tracking progress and maintaining motivation.

Activity instructions:
- **Set up your space:** Find a quiet, comfortable area where you can focus and spread out your materials. Gather your notebook or journal, sticky notes or index cards, and any additional materials like a large piece of paper or coloured pens.
- **Learning goals:** Think about what new skills or knowledge you want to acquire. Learning goals focus on the process of gaining new competencies. Examples include "Learn to speak conversational Spanish" or "Develop advanced Excel skills."
- **Performance goals:** Consider what outcomes or achievements you want to reach. Performance goals are results oriented. Examples include "Complete a certification course with a grade of 90% or higher" or "Increase sales by 20% this quarter."
- **Brainstorm:** Write down you're learning and performance goals on separate sticky notes or index cards. Use one note for each goal. Ensure each goal is specific, measurable, achievable, relevant, and time-bound (SMART).
- **Create a goal map:** On a large piece of paper or poster board, create a visual map or timeline for your goals. Place your goals around the map and draw connections or paths that illustrate how you will achieve them.
- **Set milestones:** Break down each goal into smaller milestones or steps. Write these milestones on additional sticky notes or index cards and place them on the map. For example, if your goal is to "Learn to speak conversational Spanish," milestones might include "Complete beginner's course" and "Practice speaking with a native speaker."

- **Set review dates:** Decide on specific dates to review your progress. Mark these dates on your calendar or include them on your goal map. After completing milestones, take time to reflect on what you've achieved, and any adjustments needed. Write down your reflections and any new insights in your notebook.
- **Commit and share:** Make a personal commitment to work towards your goals. Write a brief statement of commitment in your journal. If comfortable, share your goals and map with a friend, mentor, or accountability partner. Discuss how you plan to achieve your milestones and seek their support or feedback.

Alternative activities:
- **Vision board:** Create a vision board with images, words, and symbols representing your goals. Place it where you can see it daily to keep you motivated.
- **Check-in app:** Use a goal setting or tracking app to digitally track your progress and set reminders for your milestones.

Reflection:
- How clear and specific are your learning and performance goals? Did breaking them down into milestones help?
- How did mapping out your goals and milestones impact your motivation and commitment?
- What additional steps can you take to stay on track with your goals and continue making progress?

Embracing wholeness: Accepting your authentic self

Authenticity is the practice of being true to oneself by embracing your values, beliefs, and feelings without pretence. This fosters genuine connections, leading to enhanced self-fulfilment and confidence, which are crucial for mental health and overall well-being. The science behind authenticity suggests that living in alignment with one's true self can reduce stress and anxiety, as it minimizes cognitive dissonance and promotes self-acceptance.

Time: 45–60 minutes
Location: A quiet and comfortable space
You will need:
- A notebook or journal
- Pens or markers
- Mirrors or reflective surfaces (optional)
- A computer or device for additional resources (optional)

You will learn:
- How to identify and accept different aspects of your authentic self.
- Techniques for integrating your strengths, values, and vulnerabilities into a cohesive sense of self.
- Strategies for fostering self-compassion and embracing your whole self.

Activity instructions:
- **Introduction to authenticity:** The importance of accepting and integrating all aspects of yourself matters for your well-being. Being authentic involves

recognizing both strengths and vulnerabilities to create a complete sense of self.

- **Identify core aspects:** Reflect on the key aspects of who you are, including your strengths, values, passions, and vulnerabilities. Write down these aspects in your journal. Think about how these aspects contribute to your sense of authenticity. How do they define who you are and influence your actions and decisions?

- **Mirror exercise:** Stand in front of a mirror or use a reflective surface. Take a few moments to look at yourself and acknowledge both your physical appearance and inner qualities. Reflect on what you see and how it aligns with your sense of authenticity. Write down positive affirmations related to your authentic self. These can include acknowledging your strengths, values, and the acceptance of your vulnerabilities.

- **List strengths and vulnerabilities:** In your journal, create two columns – one for your strengths and one for your vulnerabilities. List out what you see in each category. Write about how your strengths and vulnerabilities interact and contribute to your sense of self. How do they help you grow and understand yourself better?

- **Acceptance exercise:** Reflect on any areas where you might struggle with acceptance. Consider how you can approach these areas with self-compassion and understanding.

- **Create an action plan:** Based on your reflections, set specific goals for embracing and expressing your authentic self. These goals might include practicing self-compassion, engaging in activities that reflect your values, or addressing areas where you struggle with acceptance. Outline practical steps to achieve these goals. Consider how you will integrate these practices into your daily life and monitor your progress.

- **Journal your insights:** Write down your final thoughts on how accepting your authentic self contributes to your sense of wholeness. Reflect on any new insights or shifts in perspective.

Alternative activities:

- **Letter to your younger self:** Write a compassionate letter to your younger self, addressing moments when you felt misunderstood or disconnected from your true self. Offer encouragement and support, helping your past self embrace wholeness.
- **Authenticity check-ins:** Regularly check in with yourself to assess how well you are embracing and expressing your authentic self. Adjust your action plan as needed.

Reflection:

- How did reflecting on your strengths, vulnerabilities, and overall sense of self contribute to your understanding of your authenticity?
- What changes or insights did you gain from integrating different aspects of yourself into a cohesive sense of self?
- How do you anticipate your goals and action steps will help you embrace and express your authentic self in your daily life?

Milestone mosaic: Crafting your personal growth timeline

Achievement encompasses the pursuit and attainment of goals that foster a sense of accomplishment and competence. Striving for mastery and success not only enhances self-esteem but also contributes significantly to personal growth and overall life satisfaction, playing a vital role in long-term well-being and fulfilment. Pursuing and reaching goals cultivates a sense of competence and mastery, which can lead to increased positive emotions and greater resilience. This process enhances one's engagement in activities and relationships, as success can inspire further efforts. Furthermore, the act of achieving goals can provide a sense of purpose and meaning in life, reinforcing the idea that one's efforts contribute to personal and societal betterment.

Time: 60–90 minutes
Location: A comfortable indoor space with enough room to spread out materials
You will need:
- A large piece of paper or poster board
- Coloured pens or markers
- Sticky notes
- Glue or tape
- Scissors

You will learn:
- How to visually map significant life events that have contributed to your personal growth.
- Techniques for reflecting on past experiences and their impact on your current self.

- Insights into potential future directions based on past experiences and lessons learned.

Activity instructions:
- **Set up your space:** Find a comfortable, well-lit area where you can work freely. Ensure you have enough space to spread out your materials. Gather your large paper or poster board, coloured pens or markers, sticky notes or index cards, and any additional decorative elements if desired.
- **Draw the timeline:** On your large piece of paper or poster board, draw a horizontal line across the centre to represent the timeline of your life. Label one end as "Beginning" and the other end as "Present" or "Current day."
- **Mark key events:** Identify significant achievements, disappointments, life-changing situations, or any events that have contributed to your growth. Write each event on a separate sticky note. Place them along the timeline in chronological order.
- **Add details:** Use coloured pens or markers to draw symbols, doodles, or illustrations that represent each event. Add personal touches to enhance the visual impact of your timeline.
- **Highlight milestones:** Use different colours or decorative elements to highlight particularly significant events. This could include achievements, challenges, and turning points.
- **Identify patterns:** Write reflections in your journal about each key event on your timeline. Consider how each event contributed to your personal growth and what lessons you learned. Look for patterns or recurring

themes in your timeline. Note any common threads in your experiences or growth areas.
- **Envision your future:** On the right side of your timeline (beyond the present day), draw or write about future aspirations, goals, or dreams. Visualize how you hope your journey will continue and what milestones you aim to achieve.
- **Plan for growth:** Based on your reflections, identify potential areas for future growth. Consider how you can apply lessons from past experiences to new challenges or opportunities.
- **Share your journey:** Take a final look at your completed timeline. Reflect on the overall journey and how it has shaped who you are today. If comfortable, share your timeline with a trusted friend, family member, or mentor. Discuss your reflections and future aspirations with them for additional insights and support.

Alternative activities:
- **Life chapters timeline:** Create a timeline of your life, dividing it into "chapters" based on meaningful periods. Reflect on how each chapter contributed to your personal growth.
- **Strengths journey map:** Draw a map illustrating moments when your core strengths helped you grow. Focus on how your unique qualities shaped the path you've taken.

Reflection:
- What did you learn about your personal growth from creating your timeline?

- Did you notice any patterns or recurring themes in your experiences? How have these shaped your growth?
- How can you use your past experiences to inform and guide your future goals and aspirations?

Section II

Nature-Based Interventions

Nature connectedness

In today's fast-paced world, many of us are increasingly disconnected from the natural environments that once played a central role in our lives. Sedentary lifestyles, driven by prolonged screen time and urban living, contribute to a growing detachment from nature. This disconnect not only impacts our physical health but also our mental and emotional well-being. As we spend more time indoors and less time interacting with the natural world, we miss out on the profound benefits that nature offers.

Nature connectedness refers to a deep sense of belonging and relationship with the natural world, fostering well-being and physical health. This section of the book delves into the scientific principles underlying nature connectedness, including the biophilia hypothesis, stress reduction theory (SRT), and attention restoration theory (ART). Additionally, it introduces the five pathways – senses, beauty, emotion, meaning, and compassion for deepening our relationship with the natural world.

The biophilia hypothesis, posits that humans have an intrinsic affinity for nature. This deep-seated connection is rooted in our evolutionary history, and interacting with nature satisfies a fundamental need, promoting psychological and physiological well-being. Wilson's hypothesis underscores the vital role of nature in our overall health and happiness, emphasizing that our connection to the natural world is crucial for a fulfilling life.

Stress reduction theory (SRT), highlights nature's unique ability to alleviate stress. According to SRT, natural environments provide a critical respite from daily pressures, leading to reduced stress levels and improved well-being. The calming effects of nature contribute to lower physiological stress markers, such as heart rate and blood pressure, and elevate mood, making nature an essential tool for stress management.

Attention restoration theory (ART), focuses on the cognitive benefits of nature. ART suggests that natural settings are particularly effective in restoring our attentional capacities. Unlike urban environments that demand continuous directed attention, nature engages our involuntary attention, allowing our cognitive resources to recuperate. This effortless engagement enhances mental clarity and cognitive resilience.

To facilitate a deeper engagement with nature, the five pathway model provides a structured approach. This model identifies five pathways that offer unique opportunities for enhancing our connection with the natural world.

- **Senses:** Engaging our senses is fundamental to deepening our connection with nature. Activities that stimulate sensory experiences, such as feeling the texture of tree bark or basking in sunlight, enhance our awareness and appreciation of the natural world. This pathway involves immersing ourselves in the sights, sounds, smells, and textures of nature to foster a deeper sensory connection.
- **Beauty:** Appreciating the aesthetic qualities of nature has a profound impact on our well-being. Observing nature's beauty through activities like photography or creating nature mandalas allows us to focus on and celebrate nature's visual splendour. This pathway emphasizes the role of nature's beauty in enhancing our emotional and cognitive responses.

- **Emotion:** Nature has the power to evoke and regulate our emotions. Engaging in practices that connect us emotionally with nature, such as listening to birdsong or stargazing, facilitates emotional restoration and fosters positive feelings. This pathway focuses on how nature influences our emotional states and helps us find awe and calm.

- **Meaning:** Finding meaning in our interactions with nature enriches our sense of purpose and belonging. Participating in activities like eco-challenges or reflecting on nature's wisdom helps us connect with a greater sense of purpose and understand our place within the natural world. This pathway highlights the significance of nature in enhancing our sense of meaning and satisfaction.

- **Compassion:** Developing compassion for the environment fosters a sense of responsibility and connection. Activities that promote environmental stewardship, such as making eco-friendly commitments or collecting nature mementos, encourage us to care for and reflect on our role within the natural world. This pathway nurtures a compassionate relationship with nature and reinforces our commitment to sustainability.

This section of the book presents a variety of activities designed to enhance nature connectedness through these pathways. Each activity is crafted to help you explore and deepen your relationship with the natural world, offering opportunities for personal growth and renewal. By incorporating these practices into your life, you can experience the many benefits of nature connectedness to cultivate a more fulfilling and balanced life.

Nature fix: Quick breaks in nature

Nature connectedness is the feeling of belonging and relationship with the natural world. It promotes well-being by reducing stress and fostering emotional resilience, supported by research showing that exposure to nature improves recovery from work stress. Studies using environmental and work psychology frameworks have demonstrated that even short breaks in nature enhance recovery, reduce cortisol levels, and boost creativity and job performance.

Time: 5–10 minutes

Location: Anywhere you like during the day – home, office, public transport, etc.

You will need:

- A small container or bag for nature items (optional)

You will learn:

- To notice and appreciate small elements of nature in your environment.
- How to use brief, creative moments to reduce stress and refresh your mind.
- How to incorporate nature connection into your daily routine seamlessly.

Before you begin:

- If possible, carry a small container or bag for collecting tiny natural items (e.g., leaves, pebbles).

Activity instructions:

- **Notice nature on the go:** As you move through your day, take a few moments to look around for small elements of nature – whether it's a flower growing through the cracks of the sidewalk, a tree outside your window, or a patch of greenery in your environment.

- **Pause and appreciate:** When you notice something interesting in nature, stop for a moment to focus on it. Take in the details, like the vibrant colours, the textures of a leaf, the scent of flowers, or the sounds of rustling leaves or birds. Let your senses fully engage with the moment.
- **Engage your senses:** If it's safe and respectful to do so, gently touch the natural object – a leaf, a pebble, or a flower. Feel its texture, weight, or softness. Observe its unique features and appreciate its presence. Allow your eyes to linger on it and take a mental snapshot of the details, such as the shades of green in the leaves or the intricate pattern of veins on a petal.
- **Reflect and breathe:** Take a few deep breaths, letting your body relax. Reflect on how engaging with nature makes you feel – whether it calms your mind, lifts your mood, or helps you feel grounded. Notice any shifts in your emotions or stress levels. Acknowledge the sense of peace that arises from this brief connection.
- **Carry nature with you:** If you collected a small natural item (like a pebble or a leaf), keep it with you as a reminder of your connection to the natural world. Whenever you feel stressed or distracted, holding or looking at the item can help you reconnect.

Alternative activities:
- **Daily nature reminder:** Set a daily reminder on your phone to prompt you to take a quick break to step outside for a breath of fresh air. Notice how the outdoor environment feels – whether it's the temperature, sounds, or smells – to reconnect with nature.

- **Pause to look outside:** Take a break from your screen and spend a few moments gazing out of your window. Notice the details of nature – trees, clouds, birds, or passersby – to refresh your mind.

Reflection:
- How did taking a quick nature break impact your mood or stress levels?
- Did noticing and capturing nature help you feel more connected to your surroundings?
- How can you integrate this practice into your routine to make it a regular part of your day?
- What other creative ways can you explore to connect with nature on the go?

Birdsong musings: Tune into nature's symphony

Listening to birdsongs significantly contributes to well-being by promoting relaxation and reducing stress. A recent study found that listening to birdsongs can improve mood and decrease feelings of anxiety. The soothing and natural sounds foster a deeper connection with nature, enhancing peace of mind. This sensory engagement not only inspires feelings of joy and tranquillity but also supports mental health by boosting emotional resilience and improving overall cognitive function.

Time: 15–20 minutes
Location: A quiet outdoor space with birds, such as a park, garden, or near a window
You will need:
- A comfortable spot to sit or lie down
- A journal for reflection (optional)

You will learn:
- How to develop your ability to focus on the soothing sounds of bird songs and nature.
- How to foster a deeper sense of peace and connection with the natural world.
- How to use the practice of focused listening to calm your mind and reduce stress.

Before you begin:
- Find a location where you can comfortably sit or lie down, ideally somewhere you can hear birds singing. Parks, gardens, or even a backyard can work well.
- Turn off your phone or put it on silent mode, minimizing distractions during your meditation.
- Take a few deep breaths to relax your body and mind, preparing yourself to be fully present in the moment.

Activity instructions:

- **Settle into your space:** Find a comfortable seated position on the ground, on a bench, or on a blanket. If you prefer, you can lie down and close your eyes. Begin by grounding yourself in your environment. Feel the surface beneath you and the air around you. Let your body relax as you settle into stillness.

- **Open your senses:** Take a few slow, deep breaths, and allow your attention to shift from your body to the natural environment. Begin to focus on the sounds around you. Notice any birds singing in the distance or nearby. You might hear chirps, calls, or whistles. Let your awareness gently expand to take in these sounds.

- **Focus on birdsong:** As you listen, allow the bird songs to become the centre of your attention. Imagine each bird's song as part of a natural symphony, unique and soothing. Don't try to label or analyse the sounds. Instead, simply notice them as they are. Observe the rhythm, pitch, and pauses between calls. Allow the bird songs to draw your attention fully into the present moment. If your mind wanders, gently bring it back to the bird sounds, using them as an anchor for your attention.

- **Tune into the environment:** After a few minutes, expand your awareness to include other natural sounds around you: the rustle of leaves, the wind, or distant sounds of water. Allow these elements to blend with the bird songs, forming a soundscape that enhances your sense of connection with nature. Stay with these sounds for several minutes, letting them guide you deeper into a state of relaxation and calm.

- **Reflect on the experience:** Once you feel ready to conclude the meditation, slowly bring your awareness back to your body. Notice how you feel – perhaps calmer, more centred, or more connected to your surroundings. Open your eyes (if closed) and take a few deep breaths before you move.

Alternative activities:
- **Birdwatching:** Spend time observing birds in their natural habitat. Bring binoculars and a notebook to jot down the species you see and their behaviours, deepening your connection to the environment and its inhabitants.
- **Flowing water:** Sit by a stream or fountain, close your eyes, and focus on the sound of flowing water. Breathe deeply, letting the soothing rhythm wash away stress and promote relaxation.

Reflection:
- How did focusing on bird songs impact your sense of calm and presence?
- Were you able to experience a deeper connection with nature through this practice of mindful listening?
- Did the bird songs help you slow down time and enjoy the peacefulness of the moment?
- Can you incorporate this practice into your daily routine to nurture a sense of calm and connection with nature?

Nature photography: Capture nature's essence

Admiring nature's beauty enhances well-being by promoting mindfulness and gratitude. Taking time to appreciate natural landscapes fosters a sense of connection to the world, reduces stress, and boosts mood. Research shows that noticing nature i.e. intentionally observing and appreciating nature, even in small doses, can increase positive emotions and life satisfaction, as well as enhance social connectedness. This practice inspires awe and wonder, contributing to greater happiness and overall life satisfaction.

Time: 30–40 minutes
Location: A serene outdoor space with varied natural features such as a park, garden, or forest area
You will need:
- A camera or smartphone with a camera
- Comfortable walking shoes
- A journal for reflection or notes (optional)

You will learn:
- How to enhance your ability to notice and appreciate the details in nature.
- How to deepen your sense of connection with the natural environment through photography.
- How to use photography as a tool for self-expression and reflection on nature's beauty.

Before you begin:
- Choose a location where you feel comfortable and inspired by the natural surroundings. Parks, gardens, or woodland areas are ideal.
- Ensure your camera or smartphone is fully charged and ready to use.

- Take a few deep breaths to centre yourself and set an intention for the activity – whether it's to find beauty in small details or capture a broader landscape.

Activity instructions:
- **Settle into your space:** Find a comfortable spot to begin your walk or exploration. Take a moment to absorb your surroundings and notice what catches your eye. Pay attention to the details of the environment: colours, textures, light, and shadows.
- **Focus on details:** Start by photographing small details that intrigue you, such as the texture of leaves, patterns in tree bark, or the intricate design of flowers. Use close-up shots to capture the subtle beauty and uniqueness of these elements. Experiment with different angles and lighting.
- **Capture the bigger picture:** Move on to wider shots that capture the essence of the landscape or the overall scene. Look for interesting compositions, such as leading lines, contrasts, or the interplay of light and shadow. Take note of how the different elements in your framework together to tell a story about the environment.
- **Engage with your environment:** As you take photos, stay present and attentive to how the environment makes you feel. Let your emotions and observations guide your choices in framing. Pause periodically to appreciate what you've captured and how it reflects your experience of the natural world.
- **Reflect on your experience:** After taking photos, find a quiet spot to review your images. What elements of nature did you find most compelling? How did the act of photographing influence your connection with the

environment? Did you notice any patterns or themes in the images you captured?

Alternative activities:
- **Macro exploration:** Use a macro lens to closely examine small natural elements like leaves, insects, or flower petals. Click some photos focusing on the intricate details often overlooked.
- **Photo gallery:** Create a small gallery of your favourite photos of nature and share them with friends or family. Discuss the stories or feelings behind each image to enhance your appreciation of nature's beauty.

Reflection:
- How did focusing on nature through photography impact your sense of connection with the environment?
- Were you able to capture elements of nature that you might have otherwise overlooked?
- Did the process of taking photos help you slow down and experience the moment more fully?
- Can you integrate nature photography into your routine to nurture your creative expression and appreciation of the natural world?

Stargazing: Experience awe

Stargazing fosters feelings of awe and wonder, enhancing well-being by promoting mindfulness and a sense of connection to the universe. This practice encourages reflection, reduces stress, and inspires gratitude, helping individuals gain perspective on their lives and improving overall well-being. People who feel a deep connection to the night sky tend to experience greater mental health benefits and happiness, along with a stronger desire to protect and preserve the natural night environment. However, those in light-polluted areas often feel less connected and less motivated to engage in efforts to protect the night sky.

Time: 20–30 minutes
Location: Outdoor space with a clear view of the night sky
You will need:
- A blanket or comfortable seating
- A notebook and pen for observations

You will learn:
- How to practice being present while observing the night sky.
- How to strengthen your sense of wonder and connection with the universe.
- How to experience the profound sense of awe inspired by the vastness of the universe.

Before you begin:
- Find a quiet outdoor space with minimal light pollution where the night sky is clearly visible.
- Prepare your blanket or seating to ensure comfort during the activity.
- Take a few deep breaths to relax and clear your mind before you start.

Activity instructions:

- **Connect with the night sky:** Lay down on your blanket or sit comfortably and look up at the night sky. Take a few moments to observe the vastness and beauty of the stars. Notice the patterns and constellations if they are visible.
- **Mindful observation:** Focus on the stars and the movement of celestial objects. Pay attention to the colours, brightness, and positions of different stars. Observe how the night sky changes as time passes. If you prefer, use a notebook to jot down any thoughts or feelings that arise during your observation. Note any constellations or celestial events you find particularly intriguing.
- **Experience awe:** Allow yourself to be fully immersed in the experience. Feel the enormity of the universe and the smallness of your own presence in contrast. Let the vastness and beauty of the night sky evoke a sense of awe and wonder. Reflect on the scale of the cosmos and how it inspires feelings of amazement and appreciation.
- **Relax and reflect:** Take a few moments to absorb the experience of awe. Feel the tranquillity of the night and let it deepen your relaxation. Reflect on how this sense of awe impacts your perspective and emotional state.
- **Observe changes:** After spending time stargazing, sit quietly and notice any changes in your thoughts or feelings. Observe how the experience of awe affects your state of mind and overall sense of well-being.

Alternative activities:

- **Night silence:** Step outside on a dark night, close your eyes, and listen to the silence or the subtle sounds of

nature. Let the stillness of the night bring a deep sense of peace and grounding.
- **Moon meditation:** Sit quietly under the moonlight and focus on the moon's coolness. Take slow, deep breaths, imagining your breath syncing with the moon's gentle glow, filling you with a sense of calm and renewal.

Reflection:
- How did experiencing the vastness of the night sky affect your mood and feelings of relaxation?
- Did the sense of awe inspire any new perspectives or insights?
- How can regularly experiencing awe through activities like stargazing enhance your sense of connection with the universe and contribute to your overall well-being?

Watering houseplants: Nurture and play

House plants enhance well-being by improving indoor air quality and creating a calming environment. Caring for houseplants not only reduces stress but also promotes mental relaxation. Research shows that interacting with plants can lower diastolic blood pressure and decrease sympathetic nervous system activity, which helps reduce physiological stress. People report feeling more comfortable, soothed, and natural after tending to plants, as compared to mentally demanding tasks like computer work. This highlights the mental health benefits of integrating nature into daily life, even in the form of nurturing houseplants.

Time: 10–15 minutes
Location: Indoor space with a houseplant
You will need:
- A houseplant that needs watering
- A watering can or cup of water
- A small bowl or shallow dish of water (for water play)

You will learn:
- How to practice being present while caring for your plant.
- How to strengthen your bond with both water and plants.
- How to enjoy the calming and joyful sensations of water play while watering.

Before you begin:
- Find a quiet moment in your day. Place your houseplant in a spot where you can comfortably reach it.
- Prepare a small bowl or dish of water nearby for some playful interaction during the process.

- Take a few deep breaths to relax before you start the activity.

Activity Instructions:
- **Connect with your plant**: Start by sitting or standing near your plant. Gently touch its leaves and observe its colour, shape, and any new growth. Take a few moments to appreciate its life and presence in your home.
- **Water play**: Before you water the plant, dip your fingers into the bowl of water. Let the water flow through your fingers, feel its coolness, and notice how it moves. Playfully flick the water in the air or gently splash some drops onto the plant's leaves. Engage with the water, as if it's a playful companion in this moment of care.
- **Water the plant slowly and mindfully**: After the playful moment, pour water slowly into the soil at the base of the plant. Pay attention to the way the water is absorbed by the soil, the sound it makes, and how the plant responds. Imagine you are nourishing it with care and joy.
- **Tune into your senses**:
    - **Touch**: Feel the water in your hands and the texture of the soil.
    - **Sight**: Watch how the water glistens on the leaves and changes the appearance of the soil.
    - **Sound**: Listen to the sound of the water as it gently pours onto the plant.
    - **Smell**: Notice the fresh, earthy scent of the damp soil and the plant's leaves.
- **Express gratitude and play again**: As you finish watering, take a few moments to flick more water

playfully onto the plant's leaves, or gently pour some water over your hands, feeling its refreshment. Express gratitude to the plant for its beauty and the water for its nurturing qualities.
- **Observe the plant's response**: Sit for a few minutes observing the plant after watering. Notice how it looks after receiving water and how you feel after the playful interaction. Allow this quiet observation to calm your mind.

Alternative activities:
- **Celebrate small progress:** While watering your houseplants, observe any new growth, however small. Reflect on how, like your plants, you too grow slowly and steadily with care and attention.
- **Plant care ritual:** Dedicate a specific time each week to care for your houseplants. Use this routine as an opportunity to connect with your plants, ensuring they receive the attention they need while you enjoy a moment of mindfulness.

Reflection:
- How did the playful interaction with water change your mood during the activity?
- Did you notice any changes in your plant, and how did that make you feel?
- How can adding playfulness to routine tasks like watering a plant bring more joy to your day?

Cow cuddle: Be with a gentle companion

Connecting with animals can significantly boost well-being by promoting feelings of calm, reducing stress, and fostering a sense of grounding. Cows, in particular, possess unique behavioural traits that allow them to bond with humans, making interactions with them therapeutic and fulfilling. Animal-assisted interventions with cows have shown potential in promoting emotional balance and mindfulness, much like traditional models using dogs or cats. Cow cuddling, as a form of bovine-assisted therapy, encourages a deeper connection with nature and animals, supporting mental well-being by fostering a soothing and grounding presence. Special attention is also given to the welfare and enrichment of cows involved in these therapeutic interactions, ensuring a mutually beneficial relationship.

Time: 20–30 minutes
Location: A gaushala/cowshed with friendly cows
You will need: A safe and quiet place where cows are comfortable and calm
You will learn:
- How to connect with a cow in a calming, mindful way.
- How to strengthen your bond with nature and animals.
- How to enjoy the process of being present and embracing calm with a gentle companion.

Before you begin:
- Find a calm space at the gaushala where cows are grazing or resting.
- Take a few deep breaths to relax and focus on the present moment.

- Approach the cows slowly, respecting their space and movement.

Activity instructions:
- **Connect with a cow:** Gently approach a cow, making sure to keep calm energy and a slow pace. Allow the cow to approach you if it feels comfortable. Take a few moments to observe the cow's movements and body language, appreciating its peaceful nature. If the cow is lying down or resting, sit close by or lean against it if the cow is comfortable. Cows often enjoy being close to humans when relaxed.
- **Observe and interact mindfully:** As you sit or lie next to the cow, focus on the cow's rhythmic breathing and warmth. Notice the texture of its fur, the softness of its ears, or the rise and fall of its body as it breathes. Gently pet the cow, if it seems calm, focusing on the connection between you and the animal. Observe how the cow reacts, respecting its comfort.
- **Practice mindful presence:** Stay present in the moment by tuning into your senses. Listen to the sounds of the cow's breathing or chewing grass, feel the earth beneath you, and smell the fresh air. Allow yourself to relax and let go of any tension as you sync with the cow's calm energy.
- **Express gratitude:** Take a moment to thank the cow for sharing this peaceful experience with you. Acknowledge the role cows play in nurturing the earth and providing nourishment. Gently move away when the cow shifts its position or seems ready to continue grazing.

Alternative activities:

- **Ant trail:** Find an ant and follow its trail. Watch how it moves with purpose, working with its colony. Let the ant's teamwork and determination inspire you to think about your own goals and connections.
- **Web of life:** As you observe a bug/butterfly/ant/bird or any creature in nature, reflect on how it plays a part in the ecosystem. Think about the interconnectedness of all living beings and your own role in nature's web of life.

Reflection:

- How did the interaction with the cow affect your mood and sense of relaxation?
- Did you notice any unique details or behaviours in the cow that intrigued or calmed you?
- How can interacting with animals like cows enhance your connection to nature and well-being?

Forest bathing: Immersing in urban nature

Forest bathing, or shinrin-yoku, involves immersing oneself in nature to absorb its calming and restorative effects. This practice enhances well-being by reducing stress, improving mood, and fostering a deep connection with the natural environment. Evidence suggests that forest bathing can increase heart rate variability, a marker of well-being. Participants often report improvements in positive emotions, nature connection, and compassion while experiencing reductions in mood disturbance and rumination. These benefits indicate that forest bathing is comparable to established well-being interventions, highlighting its potential as an effective approach to enhance mental health and well-being across various populations.

Time: 30–45 minutes
Location: Urban park or green space
You will need:
- A quiet spot in the park with trees and greenery
- Comfortable walking shoes
- A guide to lead forest bathing walks (recommended)

You will learn:
- How to practice slowing down and noticing your surroundings.
- How to engage your senses to relax and reconnect with nature.
- How to build a deeper relationship with natural elements in the city.

Before you begin:
- Find a peaceful corner or path in the park where you can walk without distractions.

- Take a few moments to stand still, relax, and breathe deeply to clear your mind before starting the activity.

Activity instructions:
- **Slow down and walk mindfully:** Begin walking slowly, paying attention to each step. Feel the ground beneath your feet, noticing the rhythm of your movements. Allow yourself to move at a calm, unrushed pace.
- **Engage your senses:** As you walk, pause occasionally and focus on each of your senses:
  - **Sight:** Notice the shades of green, the light filtering through leaves, or the shapes of trees. Look closely at the details of a leaf, branch, or flower.
  - **Sound:** Listen for birds chirping, the rustling of leaves, or distant urban sounds blending with nature.
  - **Smell:** Inhale the scent of grass, flowers, or even the earth after rain. Urban parks have unique smells that connect city life with natural elements.
  - **Touch:** Gently touch the bark of a tree or feel the texture of leaves. Engage your tactile senses to feel grounded in your environment.
  - **Taste:** Notice the taste in your mouth as you breathe the fresh air. While you're not tasting anything directly, this awareness adds to the sensory experience.
- **Pause for stillness:** Find a spot to sit or stand for a few minutes. Close your eyes and take five deep breaths, inhaling deeply and exhaling slowly. Let your mind quiet down and focus on the sounds and sensations around you.

- **Notice the small details:** Look around at the smaller elements of nature that might normally go unnoticed – tiny insects, patterns on the leaves, or the gentle swaying of branches in the breeze. This attention to detail helps you deepen your connection to the environment.
- **Reflect on your connection:** As you walk back, think about how the park and nature within the urban setting make you feel. Reflect on how nature coexists with city life and what this experience brings to your sense of well-being.
- **Conclude with gratitude:** Take a moment before leaving the park to thank the space for offering you this time of peace and reflection. Take a final deep breath, feeling a sense of connection to nature in your urban surroundings.

Alternative activities:
- **Forest breathing:** Find a quiet outdoor spot. Close your eyes, take deep breaths, and focus on the subtle sounds around you – wind, birds, rustling leaves. Stay present and enjoy the stillness.
- **Being with a Flower:** Find a beautiful flower. Gently observe its colours, patterns, and fragrance. Take a deep breath and let its beauty bring a sense of calm and appreciation for nature's simple wonders.

Reflection:
- How did this urban forest bathing experience differ from being in a remote natural area?
- Did you discover new aspects of nature in the city that you hadn't noticed before?
- How do you feel now compared to when you first entered the park?

Tree hugging: Feel a deep connection

Tree hugging promotes well-being by fostering a deep connection with nature. This simple act encourages mindfulness, reduces stress, and enhances feelings of peace and tranquillity. Trees hold practical, cultural, and spiritual significance, playing a vital role in human life across urban and rural settings. Research identifies various human–tree relationships influenced by lifestyles and nature connections. For instance, people often admire large, old trees based on sensory and emotional experiences, while nurturing relationships develop with young trees in personal gardens. Nostalgic connections can also arise from trees that hold symbolic value in memories. Ultimately, tree hugging can boost mood, encourage gratitude for the environment, and cultivate a sense of belonging for nature.

Time: 10–15 minutes
Location: Outdoor space with trees
You will need:
- A tree in a park, forest, or garden
- Comfortable clothing for being outdoors

You will learn:
- Practising being present with nature.
- How to experience physical and emotional grounding through tree hugging.
- How to use breathwork and sensory awareness to release tension.

Before you begin:
- Find a tree that feels inviting and peaceful to you.
- Approach the tree with a sense of respect, as though meeting an old friend.

- Take a few deep breaths and relax before you start the activity.

Activity instructions:
- **Choose your tree**: Walk around and find a tree that draws your attention. It could be its shape, size, or something that makes it feel special. This tree will be your companion for the next few minutes.
- **Prepare to connect**: As you approach the tree, place your hands gently on the trunk. Close your eyes and focus on the texture of the bark. Take a few deep breaths, inhaling through your nose and exhaling through your mouth. Let yourself relax.
- **Hug the tree**: When you feel ready, wrap your arms around the tree. Rest your body gently against it, either fully embracing the trunk or leaning your back against it.
- **Tune into your senses**:
  - **Touch**: Feel the tree's texture, temperature, and strength.
  - **Smell**: Inhale the scent of the wood, leaves, and earth.
  - **Sound**: Listen to the sounds of the wind, leaves rustling, or birds singing.
  - **Breath**: Focus on your breath, matching the rhythm of your inhales and exhales with the imagined breath of the tree.
- **Visualize grounding**: Imagine the roots of the tree spreading deep into the earth. Picture your own energy flowing down through your body and into the ground, connecting you with nature and releasing any tension or stress.

- **Stay present**: Spend the next few minutes simply being with the tree. Let your mind wander without attachment. Focus on your breath, the tree, and the environment around you.
- **End with gratitude**: After sometime, slowly release the tree and place your hands back on its trunk. Take one final deep breath and say a silent thank you to the tree for its presence and support.

Alternative activities:
- **Root connect:** Sit at the base of a tree and lean your back against its trunk. Imagine your body merging with the tree's roots, feeling anchored, calm, and supported by nature's strength.
- **Heart to bark:** Place both hands on a tree's trunk, breathe deeply, and visualize your heart energy connecting with the tree. Feel the exchange of energy – its strength and your gratitude – flowing back and forth.

Reflection:
- How did it feel to embrace the tree?
- What thoughts or emotions came up during the practice?
- Did the experience change how you feel about nature?

Play with mud: Ground yourself

Grounding involves practices that connect individuals to the present moment and their physical surroundings, enhancing emotional regulation and reducing anxiety. Techniques such as walking barefoot on natural surfaces or focusing on sensory experiences while playing with mud promote mindfulness, increase resilience, and foster a sense of stability and well-being. Emerging research highlights the potential of incorporating eco-art therapy into health care, supporting the idea that creative practices can enhance emotional well-being. By integrating these interventions across various settings, we can further promote health, illness management, and overall well-being, reinforcing the benefits of grounding techniques.

Time: 20–30 minutes
Location: Outdoor space with access to mud, clay, or dirt
You will need:
- A patch of dirt, clay, or mud (or water to create mud from dry dirt)
- A small bucket of water (optional)
- Simple tools like sticks, leaves, or stones for creative play (optional)
- A towel and water for cleaning up afterward

You will learn:
- How to be fully present and engaged with the earth's textures and materials.
- How to deepen your connection with the natural elements of the earth.

- How to experience the calming, grounding energy of working with the earth while engaging your creative side.

Before you begin:
- Choose a spot in nature where you can access dirt, clay, or mud. If you are starting with dry dirt, you can add water to create mud.
- Wear clothes that you don't mind getting dirty and prepare a towel and water for cleanup after the activity.

Activity instructions:
- **Get grounded:** Start by sitting or kneeling on the ground near your patch of dirt or clay. Take a few moments to connect with the earth beneath you. Feel its solid, grounding presence and take a few deep breaths, imagining the earth's stability and strength anchoring you.
- **Explore the texture:** Pick up a handful of dirt, clay, or mud. Focus on the texture – whether it feels gritty, smooth, cold, or warm. Slowly run your fingers through it, press it between your palms, or let it fall through your fingers. Fully engage with the sensation as you ground yourself through touch.
- **Play and create:** Using the mud, dirt, or clay, begin to play. You can mould shapes, build small sculptures, or create patterns on the ground. Let your creativity flow freely, enjoying the process of forming connections with the earth. Use natural materials around you (sticks, leaves, stones) to enhance your creations, allowing the earth to inspire a playful, grounding interaction.
- **Feel the grounding energy:** As you play, reflect on how the earth grounds and supports all life. Imagine its stable energy connecting with you through your hands.

Notice how this simple connection with dirt or clay helps you feel more rooted and present.

- **Tune into your senses:** Engage all your senses while working with the mud or clay. Feel the cool, wet texture in your hands and how it changes as you mould it. Observe the earthy colours and the way the mud or clay forms in your hands. Notice the fresh, earthy scent of the dirt or clay. Listen to the quiet rustling of leaves, birds, or your own movement as you play.
- **Reflect and clean up:** Once you're done playing, notice any sense of calm, groundedness, or connection that has emerged. Use your towel and water to clean up, feeling a sense of closure and gratitude for the grounding experience.

Alternative activities:
- **Nature imprints:** Collect leaves, flowers, or textured surfaces and press them into clay or mud to create imprints. This activity allows you to connect with nature's patterns and textures while grounding yourself in the creative process.
- **Mud painting:** Mix mud or clay with natural pigments (like crushed berries or leaves) to create paint. Use your fingers or sticks to create designs on paper or rocks, letting your creativity flow while connecting with nature.

Reflection:
- How did playing with the mud or clay affect your sense of groundedness?
- Did the texture and sensation of the earth change your mood or energy?

- How did the playful interaction deepen your connection with the earth and nature?
- Can you see yourself incorporating more earthy, grounding moments into your daily life?

Green exercising: Move, breathe, and connect

Green exercising – engaging in physical activity outdoors – enhances well-being by combining the benefits of exercise with the restorative effects of nature. This practice reduces stress, improves mood, and boosts mental clarity, fostering a sense of connection to the environment while promoting overall physical and mental health. Research examining the effects of outdoor exercise compared to indoor exercise indicates that green exercise may positively influence affective experiences and enjoyment among participants.

Time: 30–45 minutes
Location: Urban park with open green space
You will need:
- Comfortable workout clothes and shoes
- A water bottle
- A fitness tracker or stopwatch (optional)

You will learn:
- How to engage in low-impact exercise while enjoying the park's fresh air and natural environment.
- How to cultivate a deeper connection with nature through movement and awareness of your surroundings.
- How to allow nature's calming effects to reduce stress and enhance well-being as you exercise.

Before you begin:
- Choose a time when the park is relatively quiet, perhaps in the early morning or late afternoon, to avoid the busier hours.
- Warm up for a few minutes with gentle stretches or a brisk walk, allowing your body to adjust and become present in the park's atmosphere.

- Set an intention for your exercise – whether it's to improve physical health, relieve stress, or simply enjoy moving in nature.

Activity instructions:
- **Warm-up in nature:** Start with a 5-minute brisk walk around the park, taking deep breaths and noticing the natural elements around you: trees, grass, flowers, and the sky. As you walk, feel your body begin to warm up. Focus on the sensation of the ground beneath your feet, the breeze on your skin, and the rhythm of your steps.
- **Circuit of simple exercises:** Once you've warmed up, find an open space in the park where you can comfortably perform exercises. Perform the following exercises or exercises of your choice, each for 1 minute. Take a 30-second rest between each exercise:
  - **Walking lunges:** As you move forward with lunges, keep your gaze on the trees or skyline, appreciating the beauty around you.
  - **Push-ups:** Position yourself on a bench or the grass, tuning into the sounds of nature as you complete each rep.
  - **Squats:** Imagine yourself grounding into the earth with each squat, feeling your body's connection to the natural surroundings.
  - **Planks:** Hold your plank position, focusing on the steady rhythm of your breath and the calming environment around you.
  - **Jumping jacks:** Let your movements flow freely, feeling energized by the fresh air and natural space.
- **Mindful cool-down:** After the exercise circuit, slow down with a cool-down walk around the park for 5–10

minutes. As you walk, shift your awareness fully to your surroundings. Take deep, slow breaths, inhaling the fresh air, and let the movement gradually become softer. Notice the sensations in your body as it relaxes from the exercise. During this time, allow yourself to tune into the peaceful aspects of the park – maybe the rustling leaves, the distant sound of birds, or the warmth of the sun on your skin.

Alternative activities:
- **Park yoga:** Find a quiet spot in the park to practice yoga. Incorporate poses that open your senses to the surroundings, such as tree pose, warrior pose, and sun salutations, allowing the natural environment to enhance your practice.
- **Outdoor dance:** Find an open space and let loose with some free-form dancing. Play your favourite music and move with the rhythms of nature around you, connecting your body and spirit to the environment.

Reflection:
- How did exercising in the urban park enhance your physical and mental well-being compared to indoor workouts?
- Did you feel more energized, calm, or connected to nature after your green exercise session?
- How did the sights, sounds, and sensations of the park influence your mood and stress levels?
- Can you see yourself incorporating more green exercise into your routine for both fitness and relaxation?

Nature's wisdom: Finding meaning in the outdoors

Finding meaning in nature involves discovering personal significance and connection within natural environments. This process fosters reflection, a sense of belonging, and enhances positive rumination. Research highlights that connecting with nature is a pathway to discovering meaning in life, addressing our needs for coherence, significance, and purpose. Nature serves as a common source of meaning for many individuals, enriching their appreciation for life experiences. Engaging with the natural world can inspire gratitude, promote well-being, and encourage deeper insights into life's purpose, contributing to overall happiness and fulfilment.

Time: 30–45 minutes
Location: A natural setting such as a park, forest, or garden
You will need:
- A journal or sketchbook
- A pen or pencils
- A small nature item for inspiration (e.g., a leaf, rock, or flower) (optional)

You will learn:
- How to discover personal meaning and reflections through direct engagement with nature.
- How to enhance your ability to notice and interpret natural elements meaningfully.
- How to use creative methods to articulate your thoughts and feelings about nature.

Before you begin:
- Choose a natural setting that you find calming or inspiring. It could be a nearby park, a quiet corner of

your garden, or any place where you feel connected to nature.

- Bring your journal or sketchbook and any optional nature item you'd like to use as inspiration.

Activity instructions:

- **Ground yourself:** Find a comfortable spot in your chosen natural setting where you can sit or lie down. Take a few deep breaths to relax and centre yourself. Close your eyes for a moment, and then open them, allowing your senses to fully engage with the surroundings.
- **Observe and connect:** Take a few minutes to observe the details around you. Notice colours, textures, shapes, and movements in the natural environment. Focus on one or more elements that capture your attention. It could be a particular plant, a rock formation, or the play of light and shadow.
- **Reflect on meaning:** Begin writing or sketching in your journal about what you are observing. Reflect on questions such as:
    - What feelings or thoughts does this natural element evoke?
    - How does this element connect to your own life or experiences?
    - What does this element symbolize or represent to you?

    If you brought a small nature item, you might use it as a focal point for deeper reflection. Consider how its characteristics relate to your personal journey or current life situation.
- **Creative expression:** Express your reflections creatively. Write a poem or a short narrative inspired

by your observations. Create a drawing or painting that represents the meaning you've found in the natural element. Develop a metaphor or story that connects the natural element to your personal experiences.

- **Integrate and reflect:** After you've completed your reflections, take a moment to think about how the insights you've gained might apply to your daily life or personal growth. Consider ways to integrate this newfound meaning into your routine, such as through mindful practices or changes in perspective.

Alternative activities:
- **Connect through narratives:** In small groups, find a quiet outdoor space at night and share stories or lessons learned from nature. Whether personal experiences or folklore, this activity deepens your connection to the outdoors and to each other.
- **Seek insights:** Take a slow, mindful walk in a natural setting. As you walk, reflect on a personal challenge or question, allowing nature's sights and sounds to inspire insights and clarity.

Reflection:
- How did focusing on a specific natural element help you find personal meaning or insight?
- What new perspectives or feelings emerged from your reflections?
- How can you continue to explore and find meaning in nature as part of your personal growth?

Picnic in nature: Slow down to savour

Recreation in nature enhances well-being by promoting physical activity, reducing stress, and fostering a sense of connection to the environment. Systematic reviews show that nature-based recreation, such as hiking or biking, is linked to significant mental health benefits, including improved mood, cognition, and emotional restoration. Engaging in outdoor activities encourages mindfulness, reduces symptoms of anxiety and depression, and supports overall mental health and life satisfaction. This highlights nature-based recreation as a promising alternative approach for improving mental well-being across diverse populations.

Time: 1–2 hours
Location: Nature park, urban park, or your home garden
You will need:
- A picnic blanket or mat
- A basket of your favourite fresh fruits
- A book that brings you joy or relaxation

You will learn:
- How to slow down and enjoy the simple, serene moments in nature.
- How to experience the tranquillity of nature through the taste of fruits, the sound of music, and the joy of reading.
- How to allow the serene surroundings to relax and refresh you.

Before you begin:
- Choose a peaceful spot in a nature park, urban park, or your home garden where you can lay out your picnic

blanket. Find a place that feels calm and where you can take in the beauty of nature.

- Pack your favourite seasonal fruits, a book, and a portable music device if you'd like to add soft, serene music to the experience.
- Take a moment to breathe deeply, preparing yourself to let go of the rush and enjoy the peaceful, slow-paced time in nature.

Activity instructions:

- **Set up your serene space:** Lay your blanket in a spot that feels peaceful and offers a good view of nature – perhaps under a tree, near flowers, or beside a stream. Let the setting itself invite serenity. Arrange your fruits, book, and music in a way that feels relaxed and accessible.
- **Pause and embrace the serenity:** Sit quietly for a few moments, simply observing the environment. Notice the stillness or the gentle movement of the trees and the breeze. Allow yourself to soak in the peaceful atmosphere and slow down the pace of your thoughts. Breathe deeply, acknowledging that this time is meant for you to savour and enjoy.
- **Savor the fruits slowly:** Begin by selecting a piece of fruit. Eat slowly and mindfully, appreciating the texture, sweetness, and freshness. With each bite, reflect on how the simplicity of nature's gifts can be savoured fully when we slow down. Consider how the earth has nurtured this fruit to ripeness, and let the act of eating be a quiet, serene connection with the natural world.
- **Immerse in your book:** Open your book and allow yourself to get lost in its pages. Let the experience

of reading in a calm, natural setting enhances your enjoyment. Take breaks between reading to look up at your surroundings, letting the peaceful environment sink in. This can help you appreciate both the world of the book and the world of nature in a balanced, slow manner.

- **Reflection and relaxation:** Once you've enjoyed your fruits and book, take a few minutes to lie back or sit in stillness. Close your eyes if you like and focus on how peaceful and calm you feel after spending this serene time in nature. Let your mind wander or simply rest, allowing yourself to truly appreciate the slow, peaceful rhythm of time spent in nature.

Alternative activities:
- **Sip and share:** Gather natural elements (like flowers and leaves) and set up a whimsical tea party outdoors. Brew herbal tea from foraged ingredients like Tulsi, mint, or enjoy your favourite milk tea, savouring the moment with friends or alone.
- **Share nature tales:** Find a comfortable spot to sit, read a book, or share stories with friends or family. Let the sounds of nature enhance the experience, creating a peaceful atmosphere for storytelling and connection.

Reflection:
- How did slowing down and enjoying serenity in nature affect your mood or energy?
- What stood out to you about the experience of combining fruits, books, and nature?
- How did the quiet moments allow you to feel more connected to the peacefulness around you?
- Can you see yourself returning to this serene practice regularly to rejuvenate and slow down?

Nature mandala: Express love for earth

Creating a mandala using nature's elements fosters joy, creativity, and self-expression, offering therapeutic benefits. Engaging in this practice encourages a deep connection with nature, promoting relaxation, emotional healing, and stress reduction. The mindful arrangement of natural materials enhances focus, presence, and emotional balance, which can lead to reduced psychological stress, improved mood, and lower cortisol levels. This activity cultivates a sense of peace and balance, contributing to overall well-being, especially for individuals dealing with physical and emotional challenges.

Time: 30–40 minutes

Location: Outdoor space with access to natural materials (leaves, stones, flowers, sticks, etc.)

You will need:

- A collection of natural elements (leaves, stones, flowers, sticks, seeds, etc.)
- A flat surface (ground or large piece of paper)
- Camera to photograph the mandala afterward (optional)

You will learn:

- How to practice being present while crafting a natural mandala.
- How to strengthen your bond with nature by using its elements as art.
- How to use the mandala as a symbol of your love and respect for the natural world.

Before you begin:

- Find a quiet, natural space where you can gather materials and create your mandala.

- As you collect natural elements, do so mindfully – gather only what has already fallen or is abundant to avoid harming the environment.

Activity instructions:
- **Gather natural materials:** Begin by walking around your chosen area, collecting a variety of natural elements like leaves, flowers, seeds, stones, or sticks. As you gather, reflect on how each item is a gift from nature. Take care to gather sustainably – use what has already fallen and avoid disturbing living plants or animals.
- **Prepare your space:** Choose a flat area where you can easily place your collected materials. This could be directly on the ground. Make sure the space allows for a circular shape, which is the foundation of the mandala. Sit in this space, take a few deep breaths, and centre yourself in the moment.
- **Create your mandala:** Start from the centre and work outward, arranging the natural elements in circular, repeating patterns. This could involve layering leaves, placing stones in a circle, or alternating between flowers and sticks. As you place each piece, reflect on how nature sustains and nurtures all life.
  Express your love and respect for the natural world by arranging each element with care and intention. Let your creativity flow – there's no right or wrong way to make a mandala. Focus on balance, symmetry, and the beauty of the elements.
- **Express love for nature:** As you create, think of the mandala as a visual symbol of your love and appreciation for the earth. Each piece you place can represent something about nature that you cherish –

whether it's the way trees provide shade, the beauty of flowers, or the way stones form the foundation of the earth. Consider saying a silent or spoken gratitude to nature for the materials you're using and for the grounding presence of the natural world.

- **Pause and reflect:** Once your mandala is complete, sit back and admire the patterns and colours. Notice the harmony in how these natural elements come together. Reflect on your connection to nature and how it supports your well-being. If you feel moved, offer a few words or a silent affirmation of gratitude for the gifts of the earth.
- **Take a photograph:** Take a photograph of your mandala to capture the moment. This can be a reminder of your love for nature and the beauty of creating with natural elements.

Alternative activities:
- **Paint nature's messages:** Collect smooth stones and paint them with words or symbols that express your love for nature. Arrange the stones in a circle or another meaningful shape, creating a mandala of gratitude and appreciation.
- **Assemble your earth art**: Gather natural materials like leaves, flowers, twigs, and pebbles. Create a collage on a canvas or large piece of paper, arranging the materials in a design that represents your personal connection to nature.

Reflection:
- How did creating the mandala help you express your love for nature?

- What natural elements were you most drawn to, and why?
- How did working with natural materials deepen your connection with the earth?
- Can you see yourself making mandalas regularly as a way to stay connected with nature?

Nature's souvenirs: A piece of
beauty from every trip

Collecting nature's treasures – such as leaves, stones, or flowers – fosters a closer connection to the environment, encouraging active engagement and appreciation for nature's beauty and diversity. This simple yet mindful interaction with nature enhances well-being by promoting creativity, joy, and a sense of accomplishment. Research suggests that engaging in these activities deepens nature connectedness, which plays a significant role in inspiring pro-nature conservation behaviours. By cultivating a more personal relationship with the natural world, this practice contributes to overall mental health and well-being, reinforcing the importance of conservation efforts.

Time: Ongoing throughout your travels
Location: Any travel destination
You will need:
- A small collection box or jar
- A notebook or digital device for recording

You will learn:
- How to create lasting memories of your travels through meaningful nature elements.
- How to enhance your connection with the places you visit by bringing back a piece of their natural beauty.
- How to reflect on your travel experiences and the natural environments you encounter.

Before you begin:
- Choose a small, portable container that you can use to collect and store your nature mementos. This could be

a box, jar, or any small vessel that fits easily in your luggage.

- Prepare a notebook or digital device to record details about each nature element you collect.

Activity instructions:

- **Collect nature elements:** During your travels, look for small, non-invasive nature elements that you can collect. These could include:
  - A unique leaf
  - A smooth pebble or small stone
  - A piece of driftwood
  - A flower petal or dried flower
  - A small seed or cone

Be mindful of local regulations and environmental guidelines. Ensure that you are not disturbing or removing protected or endangered species.

- **Record your experience:** After collecting a nature element, use your notebook or digital device to jot down or record the following information:
  - Location and date of collection
  - Description of the element (appearance, texture)
  - Any memorable experiences or observations related to the place where you found it

- **Create a nature memory collection:** Store your collected nature elements in your chosen container. Arrange them in a way that feels meaningful to you, such as by destination or by type of element. Label or tag each item with details from your recordings to keep track of where and when you collected it.

- **Reflect on your collection:** Periodically review your nature memory collection. Reflect on the experiences and places associated with each element. Consider

creating a display box for your collection if you'd like to showcase it.
- **Share and inspire:** Share your nature memento collection with friends or family to inspire them to connect with nature in their travels.

Alternative activities:
- **Memory box:** Designate a special box for storing small items collected during your trips, such as pebbles, shells, or feathers. Organize them by location or date, and revisit them to relive your experiences.
- **Support local artisans:** Purchase handmade crafts or products made from natural materials, such as wooden items, pottery, or textiles. This supports local artisans and reduces plastic waste, while also providing unique mementos.

Reflection:
- How does collecting nature elements enhance your travel experiences?
- What connections do you feel between the places you've visited and the nature elements you've collected?
- How can you use these mementos to deepen your appreciation for the natural world?

Daily eco-commitments: For a greener lifestyle

Following a greener lifestyle enhances well-being by fostering a sense of purpose and community while promoting sustainability. Engaging in eco-friendly practices cultivates mindfulness and responsibility, which can help alleviate stress and guilt related to environmental harm. Research indicates that participating in pro-ecological activities not only strengthens social connections but also boosts overall happiness and life satisfaction. These activities instil values of stewardship and encourage positive social interactions, contributing to a greater sense of fulfilment and achievement. As societies face the dual challenges of poor mental well-being and climate change, adopting a sustainable lifestyle through such communal efforts presents a promising avenue for enhancing both individual and collective well-being.

Time: 10–15 minutes
Location: Your home, office, or wherever you spend your time
You will need:
- A notebook or digital document for tracking
- A calendar or reminder app for scheduling (optional)

You will learn:
- How to increase your awareness of small, daily actions that can reduce your environmental impact.
- How to develop habits that contribute to a more sustainable lifestyle.
- How to understand how small changes can collectively make a significant difference.

Before you begin:

- Choose a specific time each day to dedicate to this activity. It could be in the morning, during a break, or before bed.
- Prepare your tracking tool – whether it's a notebook or a digital document – to record your daily micro-commitments and reflections.

Activity instructions:

- **Choose your daily micro-action:** Select one small, eco-friendly action from the following list to focus on for the day. Rotate through the actions over the week to cover different areas of environmental impact.
  - **Reduce plastic use:** Use a reusable bag, bottle, or container instead of disposable ones.
  - **Save energy:** Turn off unused lights and unplug chargers.
  - **Conserve water:** Shorten your shower time or fix a leaky faucet.
  - **Waste reduction:** Recycle or compost food scraps and avoid single-use plastics.
  - **Eco-friendly transport:** Walk, bike, or use public transport instead of driving.
  - **Sustainable choices:** Buy products with minimal packaging or those made from sustainable materials.
  - **Local support:** Buy locally grown produce or shop from local businesses.
- **Implement your chosen micro-action:** Execute your selected eco-friendly action with intention. For example, if you're focusing on reducing plastic use, make a conscious effort to avoid plastic bags and use reusable alternatives. Pay attention to how this small change affects your day and your routine.

- **Track and reflect:** After completing the action, spend a few minutes recording your experience in your notebook or digital document. Note how easy or challenging the action was, any observations you made, and how it impacted your day. Reflect on how incorporating this action into your routine affects your environmental footprint and personal habits.
- **Plan for tomorrow:** Decide which micro-action you want to focus on the next day. Set a reminder or note it in your calendar to help you remember. Consider any adjustments you might make based on today's experience to enhance your effectiveness or ease.

Alternative activities:
- **Community clean-up:** Organize a local clean-up event in your neighbourhood or park. Gather friends or community members to pick up litter, recycling materials, and beautifying the area while raising awareness about environmental care.
- **Plant-based day:** Choose one day a week to eat plant-based meals. Experiment with new recipes and ingredients, and share your culinary creations with friends to promote sustainable eating habits.

Reflection:
- How did focusing on a daily micro-action impact your awareness of environmental issues?
- Did the small changes you made feel manageable and meaningful?
- How can you integrate these eco-friendly practices into your long-term habits?
- Are there additional actions you'd like to explore to further reduce your environmental impact?

Section III

Spirituality-Based Interventions

Spiritual Practices

In our contemporary world, where the demands of daily life often overshadow our deeper pursuits, spirituality offers a transformative path to well-being and fulfilment. It is essential to understand that spirituality, as explored in this section, transcends religious boundaries. It is more about an individual's connection with the sacred and finding a sense of inner peace, purpose, and meaning in life. Spiritual practices such as yoga, pranayama, meditation, chanting, service, and silence provide meaningful ways to explore and enhance this connection. Inspired by the teachings of my spiritual master, Gurudev Sri Sri Ravi Shankar, these practices are designed to deepen our engagement with the sacred aspects of life, promote holistic well-being, and play a vital role in combating mental health challenges.

- **Yoga** is a foundational practice in many spiritual traditions, and its benefits are well-documented. This ancient discipline integrates physical postures, breathing exercises, and meditation to harmonize the body, mind, and spirit. Yoga helps cultivate physical flexibility and strength while fostering mental clarity and emotional stability. By aligning physical movement with breath and intention, yoga encourages a state of balance and inner peace, making it an invaluable tool for personal transformation and well-being.

- **Pranayama**, or breath control, is another vital component of spiritual practice. This practice involves various techniques of regulating the breath to enhance energy flow and mental focus. Pranayama helps calm the nervous system, reduce stress, and improve concentration. By mastering the art of breath control, individuals can achieve a heightened state of awareness and emotional equilibrium, contributing to overall mental and physical health.

- **Meditation** is central to many spiritual traditions and is renowned for its ability to foster inner peace and self-awareness. Regular meditation practice allows individuals to quiet the mind, observe their thoughts, and cultivate a sense of presence. This practice promotes emotional resilience, reduces stress, and enhances cognitive function. Meditation serves as a gateway to exploring deeper aspects of the self and connecting with a higher sense of purpose.
- **Ancient wisdom**, as imparted by a spiritual master like Gurudev, provides timeless insights into living a meaningful and fulfilling life. This wisdom often emphasizes the importance of self-awareness, compassion, and the interconnectedness of all beings. By integrating these teachings into daily life, individuals can cultivate a sense of inner peace, purpose, and harmony.
- **Chanting** is a practice that involves repeating sacred sounds or mantras to align with spiritual energies and enhance mental focus. This practice can elevate mood, reduce stress, and create a sense of unity with the divine. Chanting helps in centring the mind, opening the heart, and fostering a deeper connection with one's spiritual path.
- **Service**, or selfless action, is a cornerstone of many spiritual traditions. Engaging in volunteering, random acts of kindness and generosity not only benefits others but also enriches one's own life. Service fosters a sense of connection, purpose, and fulfilment, contributing to personal growth and societal well-being.

- **Silence** is a profound practice that allows individuals to retreat from the noise and distractions of daily life. Embracing periods of silence offers a space for introspection, self-discovery, positive solitude, and spiritual renewal. It allows for deep contemplation and reconnects individuals with their inner selves, promoting a sense of tranquillity and clarity.

Integration of these spiritual practices into daily life enhance holistic well-being of an individual. This section of the book presents a variety of activities designed to facilitate a deeper connection with oneself and the broader spiritual dimensions of life.

Research indicates that restorative yoga including asana practice help reduce stress and improve psychological well-being by promoting relaxation and reducing anxiety. Studies on breathwork show that pranayama techniques significantly enhance focus, reduce stress levels, and increase overall vitality. Effortless meditation has been found to improve cognitive function, emotional resilience, and stress management.

Yog Nidra is associated with better sleep quality and improved emotional balance. Additionally, practices such as volunteering are linked to greater life satisfaction and mental health benefits, fostering a sense of belonging and community connection. Reflecting on essentialism, ancient wisdom, and practicing silence have been shown to promote mindfulness, reduce mental distress, and enhance emotional well-being, offering practical ways to align with deeper spiritual values.

By incorporating these spiritual practices into your routine, you can experience the profound benefits they offer, leading to a more fulfilling, balanced, and enriched life. Embracing these practices allows you to tap into a deeper sense of purpose, connect with your inner self, and cultivate a life of greater meaning and joy.

Restorative yoga: Asana flow sequence

Yoga enhances well-being by promoting physical health, mental clarity, and balance. By integrating physical postures, breath control, and mindfulness, yoga effectively reduces symptoms of depression and anxiety. Studies have shown significant reductions in depression scores and improvements in overall mental health and resilience. This practice fosters a sense of community and self-awareness, contributing to improved mood and emotional stability. Additionally, the benefits of regular yoga practice can be maintained over time, underscoring its potential as a valuable component of mental health care. Ultimately, yoga supports a holistic sense of well-being and life satisfaction.

Time: 20 minutes

Location: A quiet, comfortable space where you have room to practice yoga asanas

You will need:
- A yoga mat
- A water bottle to stay hydrated
- Comfortable clothing
- Link to guided asana sequence (preferable)

You will learn:
- How to practice gentle poses that promote restoration.
- How to enhance your awareness of your breath.
- How to integrate awareness of movement and stillness.

Before you begin:
- Set up your space with your yoga mat. Have your water bottle nearby.
- Wear comfortable clothing that allows for free movement.

Activity instructions:

- **Centring and breath awareness:** Sit comfortably on your mat with your legs crossed or extended in front of you. Close your eyes and place your hands on your knees or in your lap.

  Take a few deep breaths in through your nose, allowing your belly to expand. Exhale slowly through your mouth, letting go of any tension. Repeat for a few minutes, focusing on the sensation of your breath.

- **Gentle exercises:**
  - **Neck rolls:** Gently drop your chin to your chest and slowly roll your head from side to side. Do this for about 1 minute.
  - **Shoulder circles:** Lift your shoulders up towards your ears, then roll them back and down. Do this for a minute, then switch directions.
  - **Cat-cow stretch:** Come to a tabletop position on your hands and knees. Inhale as you arch your back and lift your head (cow pose). Exhale as you round your back and tuck your chin (cat pose). Repeat.

- **Restorative poses:**
  - **Child's pose:** Kneel on your mat and sit back on your heels. Extend your arms forward and lower your forehead to the ground. Breathe deeply and relax into the pose.
  - **Downward facing dog:** From all fours, lift your hips upward, forming an inverted V-shape. Keep your spine long, heels pressing down.
  - **Forward bend:** From downward facing dog, exhale as you step your feet toward your hands.

Slowly fold forward, allowing your head and neck to relax, settling into Standing Forward Bend.

- o **Backward bend:** Inhale, slowly roll up to standing, reaching your arms overhead. Once upright, gently arch your back, lifting your chest and extending your arms behind for a soft Backward Bend. Keep your core engaged for support.
- o **Corpse pose:** Lie on your back with your legs extended and arms at your sides, palms facing up. Close your eyes and focus on your breath, letting your whole body relax deeply.

- **Closing and reflection:** Slowly come back to a seated position. Take a few deep breaths, and gently open your eyes. Reflect on how your body and mind feel after the practice. Take a moment to express gratitude for the time you've dedicated to self-care.

Alternative activities:

- **Sun salutations:** Begin by standing tall, then gently transitioning through a series of movements that engage your body. Focus on your breath, allowing energy to flow as you clear your mind. Follow the guided instructions.
- **Spinal sequence:** Flow through gentle seated twists, lord of the dance poses, focusing on breath and mindful movement to enhance spinal flexibility and release tension.

Reflection:

- How did the restorative yoga practice impact your overall sense of relaxation and well-being?
- Did you notice any specific areas of tension or stress that were alleviated?
- How can you integrate this 20-minute practice into your regular routine for ongoing restoration?

Please scan the QR code for the link to
guided asana sequence.

Revitalizing breathwork: A pranayama practice

Pranayama, the practice of breath control in yoga, enhances well-being by promoting relaxation, reducing stress, and improving mental clarity. Research indicates that breath-based interventions can significantly reduce stress and anxiety levels while increasing emotional, social, and psychological well-being. This practice encourages mindfulness and self-awareness, helping individuals regulate emotions and enhance focus. Regular engagement in pranayama can lead to greater emotional resilience, improved physical health, and an overall sense of balance and peace.

Time: 10 minutes

Location: A quiet, comfortable space where you can sit or lie down without distractions

You will need:
- A comfortable seated or lying position.
- A timer or clock
- A cushion for added comfort (optional)
- Link to guided nadi shodhan pranayama (preferable)

You will learn:
- How to practice nadi shodhana pranayama (alternate nostril breathing) to enhance focus and relaxation.
- How to use the chosen breathwork method to reduce stress and calm the mind.
- How to develop a deeper awareness of your breath and its effects on your body and mind.

Activity instructions:
- **Settling in:** Sit comfortably with your back straight or lie down with your body relaxed. Rest your hands on your knees, palms facing the sky. Gently close your eyes and take a few deep breaths to relax and centre yourself.
- **Practice nadi shodhana pranayama:**
  - **Position your hands:** Use your right thumb to close off your right nostril. Place your right ring finger on your left nostril and your left hand on your knee in chin mudra.
  - **Inhale through left nostril:** Inhale deeply and slowly through your left nostril.
  - **Switch sides:** Close your left nostril with your ring finger and release your right nostril. Exhale through your right nostril.
  - **Inhale through right nostril:** Inhale deeply and slowly through your right nostril.
  - **Switch sides:** Close your right nostril with your thumb and release your left nostril. Exhale through your left nostril.
  - **Continue:** Repeat this process for 5 minutes, focusing on balancing and calming your breath. Aim for smooth, even inhales and exhales.
- **Conclude:** Take a few deep, natural breaths to bring your practice to a close. Pay attention to how your body and mind feel after the breathwork. Notice any changes in your energy levels or mental clarity. Gently open your eyes and take a moment to reflect on the practice or practice a guided meditation.

Alternative activities:

- **SKY breathwork:** Learn Sudarshan Kriya, which combines specific rhythmic breathing cycles to harmonize your mind and body, promoting deep relaxation and emotional balance. Daily practice of 20-minutes.
- **Brahmari pranayama:** Sit comfortably, close your eyes, and inhale deeply. Close your ears with your thumbs, hum like a bee on the exhale. Repeat for 5-10 cycles, cultivating relaxation and mental clarity through sound vibrations.

Reflection:

- How did the chosen breathwork technique impact your sense of calm and focus?
- What changes did you notice in your stress levels or mental clarity after the practice?
- How can you integrate this breathwork technique into your daily routine for sustained benefits?

Please scan the QR code for the link to
guided nadi shodhan pranayam.

Effortless meditation: Consciously relax

Meditation significantly enhances well-being by promoting awareness, reducing stress, and improving emotional regulation. Research indicates that regular meditation practice fosters self-awareness, increases focus, and cultivates a profound sense of inner peace. Participants in studies have reported greater resilience and improved mental clarity as a result of consistent meditation. This practice facilitates a deeper connection to oneself and the present moment, ultimately contributing to overall happiness and life satisfaction.

Time: 10-15 minutes
Location: Anywhere you feel comfortable
You will need:
- A quiet space where you can sit or stand comfortably
- Your intention to consciously relax for a while
- Link to a guided meditation (preferable)

You will learn:
- How to grant yourself the space to relax and unwind.
- How to use brief moments to reduce mental distress.
- How to foster a gentle attitude towards your need for rest.

Activity instructions:
- **Find your space:** Choose a comfortable position where you can sit without distractions. You can sit on a chair.
- **Take a deep breath:** Close your eyes if it feels comfortable. If not, softly lower your gaze. Take a deep, slow breath in through your nose, filling your

lungs completely. Exhale slowly through your mouth, letting go of any tension you might be holding.

- **Give yourself permission:** Silently or aloud, give yourself permission to relax. Say something like, "It's okay to take a break. I give myself permission to relax and let go for a moment." Acknowledge that taking this time to relax is beneficial and necessary for your well-being.
- **Focus on relaxation:** As you breathe deeply, imagine each breath bringing in calmness and each exhale releasing stress. Allow your mind to settle and drift. If thoughts come up, gently let them pass without engaging.
- **Brief reflection:** After a few minutes, take note of how you feel. Notice any changes in your body or mood. Slowly bring your awareness back to your surroundings. Open your eyes and take another deep breath.
- **Continue through the day:** Remind yourself that you can take these brief pauses throughout the day whenever you need them. Use these moments to reconnect with yourself and maintain a sense of calm.

Alternative activities:
- **Guided meditation:** Use a short, guided meditation app or recording if you prefer verbal guidance. You may also learn Sahaj Samadhi meditation technique – a simple yet powerful practice.
- **Sound bath:** Listen to soothing music or nature sounds, focusing on each note or sound, allowing your mind to unwind and settle naturally.

Reflection:

- How did taking a moment to give your mind permission to relax affect your overall sense of well-being?
- Did you notice any changes in your mental clarity or stress levels?

Please scan the QR code for the link
to guided meditation.

Yog Nidra: Deep relaxation for better sleep

Yog Nidra is a guided meditative practice that facilitates a state of conscious relaxation. Research indicates that this practice significantly enhances the quality of sleep by calming the nervous system, reducing stress, and promoting deep relaxation. Participants in studies have shown marked reductions in stress levels and improvements in sleep quality after engaging in Yog Nidra. This practice helps the mind transition into restorative states, leading to improved sleep cycles and a reduction in insomnia, ultimately contributing to more restful and rejuvenating sleep.

Time: 10-15 minutes
Location: A quiet, comfortable space where you can lie down
You will need:
- A comfortable lying position (savasana)
- A blanket for warmth (optional)
- A cushion under your head for added comfort (optional)
- Link to guided Yog Nidra practice (preferable)

You will learn:
- How to practice a guided Yog Nidra technique to deeply relax your body and mind.
- How to let go of stress and restore your energy through conscious rest.
- How to cultivate mindfulness and presence while allowing your body to heal and rejuvenate.

Activity instructions:
- **Preparation:** Lie down comfortably on your back in savasana (corpse pose), arms relaxed by your sides, palms facing up, feet slightly apart. Gently close your

eyes, allowing your body to sink into the surface beneath you. Breathe deeply a few times, exhaling fully to release tension. Silently set a positive intention or affirmation (e.g., "I am calm and at peace") that resonates with you.

- **Yog Nidra practice:** Begin by gently bringing awareness to your toes, then slowly move up your body, relaxing each area as you focus on it. Guide your attention from toes to head. Relax your body completely by bring your attention to your breath. Breathe naturally, without effort. Simply observe the rise and fall of your abdomen as you inhale and exhale. Visualize sensations of warmth, followed by coolness in different parts of your body. This enhances relaxation and balances energy.
- **Returning to wakefulness:** Take a few deep energizing breaths to awaken the body and mind. Slowly become aware of your surroundings. Begin to wiggle your fingers and toes, and gently stretch your arms overhead. Gently open your eyes, feeling rejuvenated and at peace.

Alternative activities:
- **Progressive muscle relaxation:** Tense and then relax different muscle groups, starting from your toes and moving up to your head, to relieve physical tension.
- **Shanmukhi mudra:** Sit comfortably, close your ears with thumbs, eyes with index fingers, nostrils with middle fingers, and lips with ring fingers. Exhale while humming like a bee, inducing deep relaxation and sensory withdrawal.

Reflection:
- How did the guided relaxation make you feel?
- What sensations or emotions did you notice during the practice?
- How can you integrate this short Yog Nidra practice into your daily routine for consistent relaxation and stress relief?

Please scan the QR code for the link
to guided Yog Nidra.

Sacred moments: Your personal
sense of the sacred

Sacredness refers to the sense of reverence and significance attributed to certain experiences, places, or practices. People can find this sense of sacredness in everyday moments, such as in nature's beauty, the creativity of art, prayers, or the tranquillity of a quiet space. By embracing the sacredness in these experiences, individuals can enhance their well-being through gratitude, fostering a deeper connection to themselves and the universe. This approach can lead to increased fulfilment, a sense of purpose, and enhanced resilience, allowing individuals to recognize the extraordinary in the ordinary.

Time: 15–20 minutes
Location: A quiet, comfortable space where you feel at ease
You will need:
- A quiet, peaceful space where you can sit comfortably
- A comfortable seat or cushion (optional)
- A journal for reflection (optional)
- An object or symbol that holds personal significance (optional)

You will learn:
- How to explore and connect with what you find sacred in your life, regardless of religious context.
- How to use a personal prayer or mantra to engage with your sense of the sacred.
- How to cultivate a sense of tranquillity and connection.

Before you begin:
- Choose a quiet space where you can be undisturbed and feel comfortable. This could be a cozy corner of your home or any place where you can relax.
- If you have an object or symbol that holds personal significance for you, place it where you can see it or hold it during the practice.

Activity instructions:
- **Ground yourself:** Begin by taking a few deep, calming breaths. Inhale deeply through your nose, allowing your belly to expand, and then exhale slowly through your mouth. Focus on grounding yourself in the present moment, feeling the surface beneath you and the air around you.
- **Introduce your sacred focus:** Reflect on what you personally find sacred or meaningful in your life. This could be a value, a relationship, a concept, or a cherished experience. Create or select a personal mantra or statement that resonates with your sense of the sacred. For example: "I honour the beauty and meaning in my life." or "I connect deeply with the essence of my values and purpose." Recite your chosen mantra or statement slowly allowing it to sink in and resonate within you.
- **Reflect and connect:** As you repeat your mantra or statement, let yourself fully experience the connection with your sense of the sacred. Notice how it feels to focus on this personal significance. If you wish, visualize or imagine something that embodies your sense of the sacred. It could be a symbol, a scene, or an abstract concept. Allow this imagery to deepen your connection.

- **Closing and integration:** When you feel ready, take a few deep breaths to gently bring your awareness back to your surroundings. If you have a journal, take a moment to write about your experience. Reflect on how connecting with your personal sense of the sacred affected your emotional state and understanding. Consider how this practice of honouring what is sacred to you can be incorporated into your daily routine to enhance your well-being.

Alternative activities:
- **Sacred moments journal:** After your practice, use your journal to explore further reflections on your sense of the sacred. Write about how this connection impacts your life and what it reveals about your values and priorities.
- **Sacred space creation:** Create a small, personal space or corner in your home that reflects your sense of the sacred. Place meaningful objects or symbols there and visit this space regularly for contemplation and connection.

Reflection:
- How did focusing on your personal sense of the sacred affect your feelings of connection and tranquillity?
- Did your chosen mantra or statement help you deepen your understanding of what is sacred to you?
- How can you integrate this practice of honouring your personal sense of the sacred into your daily life to support ongoing personal growth and inner peace?

Volunteering: Sharing your expertise

Volunteering enhances well-being by fostering meaningfulness and connection to the community. Research indicates that volunteers often report higher levels of well-being compared to non-volunteers, driven by increases in self-esteem, self-efficacy, and social connectedness. Helping others not only boosts mood and reduces stress but also cultivates feelings of gratitude and empathy. Increased social connectedness is particularly significant, serving as a vital pathway linking volunteer work to enhanced well-being. Engaging in volunteer activities can strengthen social bonds, promote meaningfulness, and ultimately lead to greater life satisfaction.

Time: 1–2 hours (initial planning and execution may vary)
Location: Flexible (online or in-person depending on the skill and recipient)
You will need:
- A list of your skills or expertise
- Access to community organizations or individuals in need of those skills
- A notebook for planning and reflection (optional)

You will learn:
- How to utilize your skills in a meaningful way to support others.
- How to connect with organizations or individuals who benefit from your expertise.
- How to experience the rewards of giving back through your unique abilities.

Before you begin:
- **Identify your skills:** Reflect on the skills or expertise you possess that could benefit others. This could

include professional skills (e.g., graphic design, writing, tutoring), personal skills (e.g., cooking, gardening, language translation), or technical skills (e.g., IT support, web development).

- **Find opportunities:** Look for local organizations, community groups, or individuals who could benefit from your skills. This can include nonprofit organizations, schools, community centres, or people in your network. Reach out to these organizations or individuals to understand their needs and how you can help.

Activity instructions:

- **Plan your skill donation:** Choose a specific skill or service you would like to offer and decide on the time commitment you are able to provide. Contact the organization or individual to discuss their needs and how your skill can be of assistance. Agree on a time and place for the skill-sharing activity.
- **Prepare your offering:** If needed, prepare any materials or resources required for your skill-sharing session. This could include creating a presentation, gathering supplies, or setting up digital tools. Plan how you will deliver your skill or service. For example, if you're offering tutoring, prepare lesson plans; if you're providing IT support, ensure you have the necessary equipment and software.
- **Execute the skill donation:** Arrive at the agreed location or set up your virtual meeting. Engage with the organization or individual and offer your skill as discussed. Be open to feedback and flexible in addressing their needs. Ensure that your contribution is practical and impactful.

- **Reflect on the experience:** After your skill-sharing session, take a few moments to reflect on the experience. How did it feel to use your skills in a volunteer capacity? What was the impact of your contribution on the recipient or organization? Did you encounter any challenges, and how did you address them?
- **Follow up and continue engagement (optional):** If you enjoyed the experience, consider making it a regular part of your routine. Look for other opportunities to offer your skills or expand your involvement with the organization. Stay in touch with the organization or individual to offer further support or explore additional ways to contribute.

Alternative activities:
- **Volunteering calendar:** Create a calendar for regularly scheduled skill-sharing sessions. This could include monthly or quarterly volunteering based on your availability and interests.
- **Skill swap group:** Organize or join a skill swap group where individuals offer their skills in exchange for learning new ones from others.

Reflection:
- How did donating your skill affect your sense of purpose and fulfilment?
- What did you learn about the needs of others and how your skills can meet those needs?
- How can you continue to use your skills to make a positive impact in your community?

No-grain day: Fruit and salad fast

Fasting can enhance well-being by promoting mindfulness, self-discipline, and a deeper connection to one's body. Research suggests that fasting encourages individuals to reflect on their eating habits, potentially leading to improved mental clarity and focus. Additionally, some people experience a sense of spiritual or emotional renewal during fasting, contributing to emotional resilience and a heightened sense of purpose. Studies have also explored the relationship between fasting, physical exercise, and sleep patterns have found it to be a valuable practice for enhancing overall well-being and longevity.

Time: 1 day

Location: Anywhere you are comfortable, ideally where you can easily access fresh fruits and salads

You will need:
- Fresh fruits (e.g., apples, oranges, berries, melons)
- Fresh vegetables (e.g., leafy greens, cucumbers, bell peppers, carrots)
- Salad dressings (e.g., lemon juice, olive oil)
- Plenty of water and herbal tea
- A journal for reflecting on the experience (optional)

You will learn:
- How eliminating grains for a day can impact your body and digestion.
- How to experience the benefits of consuming whole fruits and vegetables.
- How your body responds to different types of food.

Before you begin:
- Prepare a list of fruits and vegetables you enjoy. Plan your meals and snacks around these items.

- Ensure you are well-hydrated before starting the fast. Drink plenty of water or herbal tea.
- Set up a comfortable space where you can prepare and enjoy your meals throughout the day.

Activity instructions:
- **Morning preparation:** Begin your day with a large glass of water or coconut water. Enjoy a fruit-based breakfast. You might have a fruit salad, a smoothie made from blended fruits, or simply fresh fruits.
- **Midday meal:** Prepare a fresh salad with a variety of vegetables. Include leafy greens like spinach, add other vegetables like cucumbers, bell peppers, and carrots. Dress with a simple dressing like lemon juice or olive oil. Eat your salad slowly, paying attention to the flavours and textures.
- **Afternoon snack:** Choose a piece of fruit or a small fruit salad. This will keep you energized and satisfied until dinner.
- **Evening meal:** Prepare another fresh salad or soup, possibly incorporating different vegetables. Enjoy your salad or soup mindfully, appreciating the nourishment it provides. Continue to drink water or herbal tea.
- **Journal your experience:** After your day is complete, take a few minutes to write about your experience. Reflect on how you felt throughout the day, any changes in your energy levels, and your overall mood. Note any physical or mental changes you observed. How did eliminating grains and focusing on fruits and vegetables affect your body and mind?

Alternative activities:
- **Smoothie challenge:** Create a weekly smoothie challenge where you blend different fruits, vegetables,

and soaked nuts. Share your recipes and taste-test with friends to discover new favourites.
- **Nutritional goal setting**: Set specific nutritional goals for the month, such as increasing your vegetable intake or trying a new healthy grain. Track your progress and celebrate your achievements.

Reflection:
- How did consuming only fruits and salads for a day affect your energy levels and digestion?
- Did you notice any changes in mood or physical well-being?
- How did this experience influence your perspective on healthy eating and detoxification.

Practicing silence: Honouring your solitude

Solitude can enhance well-being by providing space for self-reflection, creativity, and personal growth. Embracing solitude allows individuals to recharge, process emotions, and practice mindfulness. This positive experience, known as positive solitude (PS), differs from simply being alone; it involves feeling meaningfully connected to oneself. Interestingly, people can experience PS even in busy places like coffee shops, where they focus on their own activities while surrounded by others. Unlike loneliness, which arises from a gap between desired and actual social interaction, PS is about our connection with ourselves. This deeper understanding can lead to greater emotional resilience and overall well-being.

Time: 10–15 minutes
Location: A quiet, comfortable space where you can be undisturbed
You will need:
- A comfortable seat or space to sit quietly
- A timer (on your phone or a watch) (optional)
- A journal for reflection (optional)

You will learn:
- How to cultivate a deeper understanding and appreciation of moments of silence.
- How to use silence as an opportunity for introspection and personal growth.
- How to develop a meaningful connection with solitude and the insights it provides.

Before you begin:
- Choose a quiet and comfortable spot where you can be undisturbed. This could be a cozy corner of your

home, a peaceful outdoor setting, or any place that feels calming.
- Set a timer if you prefer, to help you keep track of your practice time.

Activity instructions:
- **Create a comfortable space:** Arrange your space to ensure comfort and tranquillity. Use cushions or blankets to make your seat more comfortable if needed. Sit or lie down in a relaxed position. Ensure that your body is supported and at ease.
- **Deep breathing and grounding:** Begin with deep, mindful breaths. Inhale deeply through your nose, letting your belly expand, and exhale slowly through your mouth. Repeat this process for a few minutes to settle your mind and body.
- **Embrace the silence:** Allow yourself to fully experience the silence. As you sit quietly, pay attention to the stillness and the absence of external noise. Notice how the silence feels – both physically and emotionally. If your mind starts to wander, gently bring your focus back to the silence. Observe any internal noise or thoughts that arise and let them drift away without engaging with them.
- **Reflect in silence:** Use the silence as a backdrop for introspection. Who am I? What is the purpose of my life? Take a few moments to jot down any reflections or insights that arise during this practice.
- **Conclude and integrate:** When you feel ready, take a few deep breaths to gently bring your awareness back to your surroundings. Slowly open your eyes if they were closed. Take a moment to notice how you feel after the practice. Reflect on how this experience of

silence and solitude has impacted your sense of well-being and perspective.

Alternative activities:
- **Silence retreats:** Set aside a few days every year for attending a silence retreat. You may choose to attend the advance meditation program offered by the Art of Living Foundation. Being free from distractions, allow yourself to be fully present.
- **Personal reflection time:** Allocate time to sit quietly and reflect on your thoughts and experiences. Use prompts if needed, or simply allow your mind to wander, enhancing self-awareness and understanding.

Reflection:
- How did spending deliberate time in silence affect your emotional state and mental clarity?
- Did you notice any patterns or recurring thoughts during your solitude?
- How can you integrate these moments of deep silence and reflection into your weekly routine to support ongoing personal growth and tranquillity?

Essentialism: Identify what truly matters

Essentialism is the practice of focusing on what truly matters by identifying and prioritizing essential values and goals. Rooted in the ancient wisdom of aparigraha, or non-possessiveness, this approach enhances well-being by reducing overwhelm, promoting clarity, and encouraging mindful decision-making. By letting go of non-essential activities and material possessions, individuals can simplify their lives and cultivate a greater sense of purpose, satisfaction, and overall happiness. Embracing aparigraha allows for a more meaningful existence, where true fulfilment comes from appreciating what is essential rather than accumulating what is unnecessary.

Time: 45-60 minutes
Location: Quiet space with a notebook or digital device
You will need:
- A notebook or digital journal
- A computer or smartphone
- Access to digital tools (email, social media, apps)
- A timer (optional)

You will learn:
- How to identify and focus on what truly matters in your life.
- Techniques for aligning your daily activities and choices with your core values and goals.
- Strategies for simplifying your life to enhance your overall sense of purpose and fulfilment.

Activity Instructions:
- **Define your core values:** Write down your core values and principles. Consider what is most important to you

in your personal and professional life (e.g., family, health, creativity, contribution).

- **Identify long-term goals:** List your long-term goals and aspirations that align with your core values. These might include career goals, personal growth objectives, or meaningful relationships.
- **Review your schedule:** Examine your current daily and weekly schedule. Note down all your commitments, activities, and responsibilities.
- **Evaluate alignment:** Assess how each activity and commitment align with your core values and goals. Identify which ones are essential and which may be non-essential or draining.
- **Declutter and simplify:**
  - **Email management:** Organize your email inbox by categorizing messages into essential and non-essential. Delete old and irrelevant emails.
  - **Social media clean-up:** Unfollow accounts and adjust notification settings to minimize distractions.
  - **App evaluation:** Review and remove non-essential apps or tools that do not contribute to your goals.
  - **Physical space:** Go through your personal space and remove items that no longer serve a purpose or add value. Organize remaining items to reflect your core values and priorities.
  - **Mental clarity:** Reflect on your mental and emotional state. Write down any mental clutter or distractions and consider ways to address them.

- **Focus on what matters:** Use a note-taking app or planner to prioritize activities that align with your core values and goals. Schedule these high-priority activities first.
- **Establish boundaries:** Create boundaries for non-essential activities or distractions. This might include limiting screen time or setting specific times for personal and professional tasks.
- **Dedicated time blocks:** Designate specific times of the day for focused work on essential tasks or personal projects. Use techniques like time blocking to ensure uninterrupted periods for high-priority activities.

Alternative activities:
- **Daily intentions:** Start each day by setting intentions that align with your core values and goals. Write these down and refer to them throughout the day.
- **Mindful consumption:** Evaluate your consumption habits – clothing, media, food – and commit to making more intentional choices. Go for quality over quantity, choosing items that align with your values and enhance your life.

Reflection:
- How did focusing on essentialism affect your sense of purpose and fulfilment in daily life?
- What changes did you notice in your daily routine and activities after applying essentialism principles?
- How can you continue to practice essentialism to ensure your life remains aligned with your core values and goals?

Ancient wisdom: Learnings from sacred texts

Ancient wisdom encompasses teachings and philosophies from historical cultures and belief systems that emphasize holistic well-being, peace, and the interconnectedness of life. Engaging with this wisdom, particularly the higher knowledge imparted by sacred scriptures, can significantly enhance well-being by offering valuable insights into living a balanced and fulfilling life. These teachings encourage self-reflection, promote resilience, and foster a deeper understanding of one's purpose. By drawing on the profound truths found in these texts, individuals can cultivate greater life satisfaction and emotional health, aligning their actions with higher principles that guide them toward a more meaningful existence.

Time: 1 hour
Location: A quiet space for reading and reflection
You will need:
- Access to various holy books (e.g., Bhagavad Gita, Bible)
- A notebook or journal

You will learn:
- How to discover wisdom from different sacred texts.
- How to implement these quotes into your daily life.
- How ancient wisdom can influence your modern life.

Before you begin:
- Find a comfortable and quiet space where you can read, reflect, and write without interruptions.
- Ensure you have access to the holy books or reliable sources where you can find the quotes you want to explore.

- **Search for wisdom quotes:** Select one or more holy books you want to explore (e.g., Bhagavad Gita, Bible). Search for quotes or verses that resonate with you. Look for passages that offer wisdom, guidance, or inspiration. You can use online resources or physical copies of the texts. Write down your chosen quotes in your journal or on separate pieces of paper. Include the source (e.g., book, chapter, verse).
- **Personal reflection:** Take a few minutes to reflect on each quote. Consider why it resonates with you and how it applies to your life. What is the core message of the quote? How does it relate to your current experiences or challenges? What feelings or thoughts does it evoke?
- **Develop practical applications:** For each quote, write down practical ways you can incorporate its wisdom into your daily life. Consider different aspects such as personal growth, relationships, or work. Example applications:
  - **Quote:** "You have the right to perform your prescribed duties, but you are not entitled to the fruits of your actions." (Bhagavad Gita)
  - **Application:** Focus on the effort and intention behind your tasks rather than worrying about the outcomes. Practice letting go of attachment to results.
- **Create a Visual Reminder:** Use your notebook or a separate sheet of paper to create a visual reminder of how you will implement each quote. This could be a simple drawing, a list of actions, or a vision board.
- **Reflect and review:** Write a brief reflection on how exploring these quotes and developing practical applications has impacted your perspective. How do

these quotes resonate with your life and goals? What changes or actions will you take to integrate their wisdom into your daily routine? How can these insights help you navigate challenges or enhance your personal growth?

Alternative activities:
- **Wisdom circle:** Gather a group to discuss and share insights from sacred texts. Each participant selects a quote to explore, reflecting on its personal significance and how it applies to modern life.
- **Discourse exploration:** Listen to discourse that focus on ancient wisdom or sacred texts. Engage with discussions and interpretations, then reflect on how these insights can be applied to your life.

Reflection:
- How did finding and reflecting on these quotes influence your perspective on daily life?
- What practical changes or actions are you inspired to implement based on the wisdom of these quotes?

Forgiveness: Stop punishing yourself

Forgiveness enhances well-being by promoting emotional healing and reducing feelings of anger and resentment. As Gurudev Sri Sri Ravi Shankar aptly states, "Anger is the punishment you give to yourself for someone else's mistake." Forgiveness is practiced not for others but to save our mind. This spiritual practice encourages letting go of negative emotions, leading to increased happiness, reduced stress, and a greater sense of peace. Ultimately, forgiveness facilitates spiritual upliftment, enhancing overall life satisfaction and nurturing a deeper connection to oneself and others.

Time: 30–60 minutes

Location: Comfortable and private space, such as a living room or a quiet outdoor setting

You will need:

- A comfortable space
- A journal for personal reflections (optional)

You will learn:

- How to develop the ability to let go of grudges and heal from within.
- How to improve your skills in expressing feelings and understanding yourself.
- How to enhance trust and closeness in your personal relationships.

Before you begin:

- Choose a quiet and comfortable location where you can sit undisturbed. Ensure you are open to engaging in the forgiveness process.
- Approach the practice with an open heart and a willingness to engage in honest reflection.

Activity instructions:

- **Set intentions :** Sit in your chosen space and express the purpose of this individual practice: to cultivate forgiveness and strengthen your relationship with yourself. Reflect on your intention for the session, such as fostering self-compassion, healing past hurts, or deepening your inner peace.
- **Reflect on a personal grievance:** Think about a specific instance where you felt hurt or upset by someone. Journal about this experience, noting how it affected you emotionally and mentally. Write down any insights you gain about your emotions and the reasons behind them.
- **Offer forgiveness and apologies:** Express your willingness to forgive yourself or the person who hurt you. This can be done verbally or through a written note. If applicable, acknowledge any actions that may have hurt you and commit to changing those patterns moving forward.
- **Reflect and reaffirm:** Take a few moments to reflect on the experience and its impact on your feelings. Reaffirm your commitment to healing and personal growth. You might choose to write a positive affirmation or intention for future interactions.

Alternative activities:

- **Closure activity:** Write a letter to someone or a situation requiring closure, expressing your feelings, lessons learned, and intentions for moving forward. Share it in a group for support or keep it private for personal reflection.

- **Forgiveness letter:** If some people prefer not to speak directly, they can write forgiveness letters, which can be read aloud or sent as an email or shared privately.

Reflection:
- How did this process of forgiveness impact your feelings about past grievances?
- Did taking time for self-reflection help you better understand others perspectives?
- How can you continue to practice forgiveness and strengthen your relationships with yourself and others in your daily life?

Witnessing impermanence: Remembering death

Impermanence refers to the understanding that all things are transient and constantly changing, including life itself. This concept is echoed in the teachings of the Katho Upanishad, which emphasizes the fleeting nature of existence and the inevitability of death. Recognizing that death is an inherent part of life invites us to confront our mortality and appreciate the present moment. Embracing the idea of impermanence can enhance well-being by fostering acceptance, reducing attachment, and promoting mindfulness. Acknowledging the temporary nature of experiences encourages individuals to cultivate resilience in the face of challenges and find peace in difficult circumstances.

Time: 20-30 minutes
Location: A quiet and contemplative space where you can reflect peacefully
You will need:
- A notebook or journal
- A pen
- Soft meditative music (optional)

You will learn:
- How the awareness of life's impermanence can help you release attachments and focus on what truly matters.
- Techniques for letting go of fears, regrets, or attachments by contemplating the transient nature of life.
- Strategies for living more fully in the present moment with an appreciation for the fleeting nature of life.

Activity instructions:

- **Create a reflective space:** Choose a peaceful spot where you can sit comfortably and focus. This could be a serene corner of your home or a quiet outdoor space. Play soft, meditative music to help you relax and centre yourself.

- **Contemplate impermanence:** Spend a few minutes reflecting on what you would do if you had only three days to live. Knowing everything in life is temporary, including our own existence, does it changes your priorities. Consider how this awareness can influence your attachment to things, people, or situations. In your notebook, jot down your reflections on how the awareness affects your feelings about your current attachments or struggles.

- **Write a release statement:** Craft a statement or affirmation focused on letting go of attachments by acknowledging their temporary nature. For example: "I embrace the impermanence of life and release my attachment to outcomes and possessions.", "I let go of my fears and regrets, knowing that all things are transient."

- **Create a symbolic gesture:** Write your release statement on a piece of paper. Fold or tear the paper as a symbolic gesture of releasing your attachments. You may also choose to visualize this process if preferred.

- **Visualization exercise:** Close your eyes and imagine a scene where everything around you are shifting and changing. Visualize yourself letting go of attachments as you witness the ebb and flow of life's impermanence.

- **Feel the freedom:** Focus on the sense of liberation and peace that comes from accepting the transient nature of

life. Allow this feeling to permeate your thoughts and emotions.
- **Journal your experience**: Write about your experience with the contemplation of limited time, impermanence, and letting go. Note any insights, shifts in perspective, or changes in your emotional state.
- **Embrace the present:** Consider how this reflection can help you live more fully in the present moment. Write down any steps you can take to integrate this perspective into your daily life.

Alternative activities:
- **Art of letting go**: Engage in a creative activity, such as painting or journaling, focused on themes of impermanence and letting go. Express your feelings about loss and change, allowing for emotional release and acceptance.
- **Detachment journaling**: Keep a journal to explore your attachments and desires. Write about the emotions tied to them, reflecting on their impermanence. This exercise promotes self-awareness and helps you practice dispassion towards transient feelings.

Reflection:
- How did contemplating the impermanence of life impact your feelings about your attachments and struggles?
- Did the visualization exercise help you experience a sense of freedom and peace?
- How can you continue to apply the awareness of impermanence to your daily life to enhance your sense of presence and emotional resilience?

Mantra chanting: Experience positive vibrations

Mantra chanting is a powerful practice that enhances mental clarity, emotional stability, and stress reduction. Engaging in repetitive vocalization not only improves cognitive function but also positively influences emotion regulation. Individuals who regularly practice mantra chanting have reported significant enhancements in attention, working memory, and overall emotional well-being. Additionally, this practice fosters altered states of consciousness, deepening the connection between individuals and their surroundings. Ultimately, mantra chanting cultivates increased focus and mindfulness, leading to greater life satisfaction and an overall sense of well-being.

Time: 10-15 minutes
Location: Anywhere you feel comfortable
You will need:
- A quiet space where you can sit comfortably
- Your intention to consciously engage in this practice
- A link to a guided mantra chanting session (preferably):

You will learn:
- How to calm your mind by chanting mantra.
- How to focus your mind and enhance mental clarity through repetition.
- How to foster a sense of acceptance and peace within yourself.

Activity Instructions:
- **Find your space:** Choose a comfortable position where you can sit without distractions. Sitting on a cushion or chair is ideal.

- **Take few deep breaths:** Close your eyes gently or lower your gaze. Inhale deeply through your nose, allowing your lungs to fill completely. Exhale slowly through your mouth, releasing any tension.
- **Set an intention:** Silently or aloud, express your intention for this session. You might say, "I am open to clarity and peace. I embrace this moment for my mental well-being."
- **Begin chanting:** Start chanting your chosen mantra, either silently or aloud. Focus on the sound and rhythm of the words. If you have a specific mantra (like "Om Namah Shivaya"), repeat it steadily. Allow your breath to flow naturally with your chanting.
- **Focus on the sound:** As you chant, let the sound resonate within you. Picture each repetition clearing your mind of distractions. If other thoughts arise, acknowledge them and gently return to your mantra.
- **Brief reflection:** After about ten minutes of chanting, gradually decrease the volume of your voice and let the last sound fade. Sit in silence for a moment and notice how you feel. Acknowledge any shifts in your mental state or clarity. Slowly bring your awareness back to your surroundings and take a deep breath.
- **Continue through the day:** Remind yourself that you can incorporate mantra chanting into your daily routine. Use it as a tool to pause, reflect, and regain clarity whenever you feel overwhelmed.

Alternative Activities:
- **Group mantra chanting:** Participate in group mantra chanting or learn in a group. Use a short, guided mantra chanting recording for guidance.

- **Shower of mantras:** If you find it difficult to chant certain mantras, simply listen to the recordings of mantra chanting, focusing on the vibrations and allowing your mind to settle naturally.

Reflection:
- How did the practice of mantra chanting impact your overall sense of mental clarity and well-being?
- Did you experience any changes in your focus or emotional state during or after the practice?
- How can you integrate mantra chanting into your daily routine to support mental clarity?

Please scan the QR code for the link to
guided mantra chanting.

Spiritual space visit: Soak in positive energy

Sacred spaces are environments consecrated with personal significance, promoting reflection, tranquillity, and connection. Visiting these sites offers individuals an opportunity for profound transformations influenced by factors such as spirituality, culture, and the natural environment. These spaces enhance well-being by providing a peaceful retreat for prayers, meditation, and spiritual practices. Being in a sacred space fosters a sense of belonging, encourages emotional healing, and facilitates deeper connections with oneself, contributing to overall happiness and fulfilment.

Time: 1-2 hours (depending on distance and time spent at the location)

Location: A local spiritual or sacred space (e.g., temple, meditation centre, or nature reserve)

You will need:

- Comfortable clothing
- A journal or notebook
- A pen or marker
- A small token of gratitude e.g., flowers, a donation, a written note (optional)

You will learn:

- How to experience the positive energy and tranquillity of a spiritual or sacred space.
- How to cultivate mindfulness and presence in a peaceful environment.
- How to connect with your inner self and reflect on personal growth and peace.

Before you begin:
- Select a spiritual or sacred space that resonates with you. This could be a place of worship, a meditation centre, or a serene natural setting.
- Check the opening hours and any guidelines for visiting the location. Ensure you have enough time to fully immerse yourself in the experience.

Activity instructions:
- **Arrival and settling in:** As you arrive, take a moment to pause and observe your surroundings. Notice the ambiance, architecture, or natural beauty of the space. Find a comfortable spot to sit or stand. Allow yourself to relax and take a few deep breaths, letting go of any stress or distractions.
- **Explore the space:** Take a leisurely walk around the space, observing and appreciating its details. Notice any artwork, symbols, or natural features that stand out to you. Engage your senses – listen to the sounds, observe the colours, and feel the textures. Let yourself be fully present in the moment.
- **Find a quiet spot:** Choose a tranquil spot to sit quietly. It could be a designated meditation area, a peaceful garden, or any place where you feel comfortable.
  - What emotions or thoughts did you experience upon entering the space?
  - How did the environment affect your mood and energy levels?
  - What aspects of the space resonated with you the most?
  - How can you carry the positive energy and insights from this visit into your daily life?

- **Token of gratitude:** If appropriate, leave a small token of appreciation or gratitude. This could be a donation, a written note expressing thanks, or simply taking a moment to silently express your gratitude for the experience. Before leaving, take a few moments to meditate or offer a silent prayer, focusing on gratitude and positive intentions for your life.

Alternative activities:
- **Sacred object:** Choose a meaningful object to carry with you throughout your day. Pause in different locations to reflect on its significance and how it connects you to your sense of spirituality.
- **Ancestral connection:** Design a ritual to honour your ancestors or heritage. Incorporate elements that reflect your cultural background, such as traditional songs, prayers, or artifacts, creating a deep sense of connection to your roots.

Reflection:
- How did the spiritual space impact your sense of peace and well-being?
- What positive changes or insights have you gained from this visit?
- How can you integrate the positive energy and reflections from this experience into your daily routine?

Contemplation: The journey within

Contemplation involves deep reflection and thoughtful consideration of experiences, values, or concepts, serving as a pathway for spiritual enhancement. This practice promotes self-awareness, clarity, and emotional insight, which are essential for personal growth. Engaging in contemplation encourages mindfulness and helps individuals connect with their inner selves, leading to greater life satisfaction and a deeper understanding of one's purpose. Questions such as "Who am I?" and "What is the purpose of my life?", guide this journey inward, allowing individuals to align their actions with their spiritual aspirations.

Time: 30-45 minutes
Location: A quiet and comfortable space
You will need:
- A comfortable place to sit
- A journal or notebook
- A pen

You will learn:
- Techniques for deepening your understanding of your inner self and spiritual beliefs.
- How to use focused contemplation to connect with your spiritual values and insights.
- Strategies for integrating spiritual insights into daily life for greater fulfilment.

Activity instructions:
- **Create a calm environment:** Find a quiet, comfortable place where you can sit undisturbed. Arrange pillows

or a chair for comfort. Dim the lights or use a soft lamp to create a calming atmosphere.

- **Begin with grounding:** Sit comfortably with your back straight and your hands resting on your lap or knees. Close your eyes and take slow, deep breaths. Inhale deeply through your nose, hold for a moment, and exhale slowly through your mouth. Repeat for a few minutes to centre yourself.

- **Set an intention:** In your journal or notebook, write down your intention for this contemplation. This could be a question or a theme such as "finding inner peace" or "understanding my spiritual path." Keep this intention in mind as you proceed with the activity.

- **Contemplation exercise:** Select a theme or question related to your spiritual journey. This could be a spiritual concept, a personal challenge, or a value you wish to explore (e.g., compassion, forgiveness, purpose).

- **Reflect and write:** Begin writing your thoughts and reflections on the chosen theme. Allow yourself to freely explore your feelings, beliefs, and insights. Don't worry about structure or grammar; focus on expressing your inner thoughts. What does this theme or value mean to you personally? How have you experienced or practiced this in your life? What insights or realizations are emerging from this contemplation?

- **Plan action steps:** Read through your reflections and identify key insights or messages that stand out. Write down any actions you can take to integrate these insights into your daily life. This could include changes in behaviour, new practices, or setting intentions for personal growth.

Alternative activities:
- **Daily reflection:** Incorporate brief daily moments of spiritual contemplation or reflection to maintain a connection with your inner self.
- **Spiritual reading:** Choose a philosophical text that resonates with you. Spend time reading slowly, reflecting on its themes and ideas, allowing deeper contemplation to arise as you connect the text to your own experiences.

Reflection:
- How did this practice deepen your understanding of your spiritual beliefs and values?
- How can you integrate the insights gained from this contemplation into your everyday life?
- How can you make spiritual contemplation a regular part of your routine to support your personal growth and spiritual journey?

Section IV

Art-Based Interventions

Creative Expression

In the quest for a balanced and fulfilling life, creative expression emerges as an important aspect of well-being. Art-based interventions provide essential avenues for self-discovery, emotional regulation, and personal growth. Engaging in creative practices such as music, dance, visual arts, and writing has been shown to enhance emotional, social, and psychological well-being, making it a vital component of human flourishing.

Research underscores the transformative power of creative expression. One of the key theories supporting its benefits is **flow theory**, introduced by Mihály Csíkszentmihályi. This theory explains that engaging in activities that align one's skill level with the challenge can lead to a state of flow – a deeply immersive experience marked by focused attention and satisfaction. Creative activities often facilitate this state, allowing individuals to experience profound joy and accomplishment. For example, crafting, dancing, or writing can immerse individuals in a way that helps reduce stress and improve mood, promoting emotional regulation.

Expressive arts therapy provides additional evidence of the benefits of creative expression. This therapeutic approach utilizes artistic activities to help individuals manage stress, trauma, and mental health challenges. By externalizing complex emotions through visual arts, music, or movement, individuals can gain new perspectives and find relief from emotional distress. Creative activities like drawing or painting serve as powerful tools for processing and expressing emotions that might be difficult to articulate verbally, thereby aiding in emotional regulation and healing.

Emotional regulation theory, which focuses on how individuals manage and respond to their emotional experiences, further highlights the importance of creative expression. This theory suggests that engaging in creative activities helps individuals regulate their emotions by providing a structured outlet for expressing and processing feelings. Artistic endeavours allow for the externalization of emotions, which can lead to greater emotional clarity and stability. For instance, creating art or engaging in music can serve as a form of emotional release, helping individuals navigate complex feelings and achieve a more balanced emotional state.

Creative expression also plays a crucial role in **personal identity and social connection**. Art and creativity enable individuals to explore and communicate their unique experiences and perspectives. Engaging in activities such as writing a personal story or capturing moments through photography allows for meaningful self-expression and connection with others. This form of sharing can strengthen social bonds and build a sense of community, fostering mutual understanding and support.

In this section, we will delve into various creative activities designed to enhance well-being and emotional regulation. For instance, connecting with favourite songs can evoke deep emotional responses and provide solace and inspiration. Exploring inner dialogue through creative writing allows individuals to reflect on and manage their emotions more effectively. Embracing spontaneous movement in dance can promote physical vitality and emotional release, offering a way to regulate and balance emotions.

Crafting activities, such as creating personalized origami or cooking with creativity, offer tangible means of self-expression and accomplishment. Designing a small herb garden with personalized pots connects individuals with nature and encourages mindfulness, which supports emotional well-being. Visualizing well-being through drawing or capturing moments through photography facilitates personal reflection and celebrates individual achievements, further aiding in emotional regulation.

Incorporating creative practices into daily routines, such as designing personal spaces or crafting handmade gifts, enhances well-being by creating environments that reflect personal values and aesthetics. These activities foster a sense of satisfaction and harmony, reinforcing the connection between creative expression and daily life.

Overall, creative expression is more than an artistic pursuit; it is a powerful tool for emotional regulation and personal growth. By engaging in creative activities, individuals can experience profound emotional relief, self-discovery, and social connection. Embracing these practices enriches our lives and cultivates a deeper connection with our inner selves and the world around us, contributing to a more vibrant, balanced, and fulfilling existence.

Lyric resonance: Your favourite song

Music serves as a powerful tool for creative expression, enhancing well-being, and addressing mental health challenges. Research demonstrates that engaging with music can boost dopamine levels, improving mood, while reducing cortisol, a hormone associated with stress. A community-based music intervention study found that participants experienced improvements in their mental health and well-being, highlighting music's ability to foster emotional resilience and social connections among them.

Time: 20-30 minutes
Location: A quiet and comfortable space
You will need:
- A music player or streaming service
- Headphones or speakers
- A notebook or journal
- A pen

You will learn:
- How to deeply engage with the lyrics of a song to understand its emotional and personal significance.
- Techniques for exploring how music resonates with your current life experiences and feelings.
- Strategies for using music as a tool for personal insight and emotional expression.

Activity instructions:
- **Set up your listening space:** Find a quiet, comfortable space to relax and focus on the music without interruptions. Set up your music player or streaming

service and ensure you have headphones or speakers for a clear listening experience.

- **Select your favourite song:** Pick a song that holds personal meaning for you. It could be a track with lyrics you love or a song that evokes strong emotions.
- **Listen actively**
    - **Play the song:** Start playing the song and focus on listening attentively to the entire track.
    - **Focus on lyrics:** Pay special attention to the lyrics. Listen to the words carefully and try to understand the song's message, emotions, and themes.
    - **Note reactions:** As you listen, note any immediate reactions, feelings, or thoughts that arise. How do the lyrics resonate with your current life experiences or emotions?
- **Journal your thoughts:** Write down your reflections in your notebook or journal after listening. What aspects of the lyrics resonated most with you? What emotions or memories did the song evoke for you? Are there specific lines or phrases that stood out, and why? How does the song's message align with your personal values or beliefs?
- **Connect with the message:** Reflect on how the song's message or lyrics might apply to your life or personal growth. Are there lessons or insights you can draw from it?
- **Action steps:** Consider any changes or actions inspired by the song's message. How might you integrate these insights into your daily life or outlook?

Alternative activities:

- **Create a playlist:** Build a playlist of songs with meaningful lyrics that resonate with you. Use this playlist as a source of inspiration or emotional support.
- **Cultural sound exploration:** Explore music from different cultures by listening to diverse genres. Reflect on the emotions and stories conveyed, fostering cultural appreciation and broadening your perspective.

Reflection:

- How did focusing on the song's lyrics affect your understanding of the song and your emotional state?
- What personal insights or connections did you make through this activity?
- How can you use music and lyrics as a tool for self-reflection and emotional support in your daily life?

Voices within: Exploring inner dialogue

Engaging with drama – whether through participation in performances or watching plays – offers significant benefits for well-being and mental health. It serves as a powerful platform for self-expression, allowing individuals to explore and articulate their emotions in a safe environment. By immersing themselves in dramatic narratives, audience can foster empathy, build social connections, and gain insights into their own experiences. This creative engagement enhances emotional resilience and promotes personal growth, leading to improved mental health outcomes.

Time: 30-45 minutes
Location: A quiet and comfortable space
You will need:
- A journal or notebook
- A pen
- Audio recording device (optional)

You will learn:
- Techniques for identifying and understanding your mind's various voices or inner dialogues.
- Strategies for exploring how these voices impact your thoughts, emotions, and behaviour.
- Methods for integrating these insights into personal growth and decision-making.

Activity instructions:
- **Settle in:** Find a quiet and comfortable space where you can focus without interruptions. Sit comfortably with a journal or notebook and a pen. If using an audio

recording device, have it ready for recording your thoughts.

- **Identify inner voices:**
    - ○ **Close your eyes:** Begin by closing your eyes and taking a few deep breaths to centre yourself.
    - ○ **Tune in:** Pay attention to the various thoughts or "voices" you hear in your mind. These might be different perspectives, inner critics, or supportive voices. Notice their tone, content, and how they influence your thinking.
    - ○ **Record thoughts:** If using an audio recording device, start recording your immediate thoughts about these voices. Describe what you hear and how they make you feel. Alternatively, write these observations in your journal.
- **Explore each voice:** In your journal, write down each distinct voice or inner dialogue you've identified. Consider the following prompts for each voice:
    - ○ What is the content of this voice? (e.g., criticism, encouragement, doubt)
    - ○ What tone does this voice have? (e.g., harsh, compassionate, neutral)
    - ○ How does this voice influence your thoughts or decisions?
    - ○ Where do you think this voice originated from? (e.g., past experiences, societal expectations)
- **Reflect on impact:** Reflect on how each voice affects your behaviour and emotions. Are there patterns or recurring themes?
- **Reframe negative voices:** Identify any voices that are critical or negative. Write down alternative, more positive or compassionate ways to frame the messages from these voices. For supportive voices, note how you

can encourage and amplify these positive influences in your daily life.
- **Review insights:** Review your journal entries and reflections. What new insights have you gained about your inner dialogue? Write down any specific actions you can take to address or integrate the voices you've explored. This might include practices for countering negative self-talk or strategies for nurturing positive inner voices.

Alternative activities:
- **Meaningful play exploration:** Attend a performance of a meaningful play that resonates with you. Reflect on the characters' journeys and themes afterward, journaling your thoughts and emotions to deepen self-awareness and enhance your understanding of personal experiences.
- **Scene reflection**: Watch a specific scene that resonates with you. Pause and reflect on your thoughts and emotions during the performance, encouraging a deeper understanding of your inner dialogue and how it connects to personal experiences.

Reflection:
- How did identifying and exploring your inner voices impact your understanding of yourself?
- How do these voices shape your thoughts and actions, and how can you use this awareness for personal growth?
- How can you apply the insights from this activity to improve your mental and emotional well-being?

Dance of joy: Spontaneous movement

Dance is a powerful tool for enhancing well-being, combining physical movement with emotional expression. This dynamic interplay boosts mood, reduces stress, and fosters social connections. The physical activity of dancing promotes body awareness and increases endorphin levels, which are natural mood lifters. Additionally, the rhythmic and repetitive nature of dance encourages mindfulness, allowing individuals to be fully present in the moment. This holistic approach engages both the mind and body, resulting in improved mental and emotional health by helping to alleviate anxiety and depression, enhance self-esteem, and cultivate a sense of community.

Time: 20-30 minutes
Location: A spacious area where you feel comfortable to move freely (e.g., living room, dance studio, or outdoor space)
You will need:
- A music player or streaming service
- A selection of your favourite soulful songs
- Comfortable clothing
- A mirror to observe your movements (optional)

You will learn:
- How to enjoy dance without predefined steps or choreography.
- Techniques for expressing yourself through spontaneous movement.
- Developing a connection with your body and its rhythms in the present moment.

Activity instructions:

- **Prepare your space:** Find a spacious area where you can move freely without constraints. Ensure the space is safe and clear of obstacles. Choose a selection of upbeat, energizing songs that you enjoy. Create a playlist or queue up your favourite tracks.
- **Gentle warm-up:** Take a few deep breaths to ground yourself and focus on being present in the moment. Begin with some light stretching or gentle movements to warm up your body. This can include stretching your arms, legs, and torso, and doing a few light hops or gentle sways.
- **Dance freely:**
  - **Play the music:** Start your playlist and let the music play. Allow yourself to move freely in response to the rhythm and beat of the music.
  - **Spontaneous movement:** Dance in whatever way feels natural to you. There's no right or wrong way to move. Focus on how the music makes you feel and let that guide your movements.
  - **Embrace expression:** Allow yourself to express different emotions or energies through your dance. Move with joy, abandon, or any feeling that the music evokes.
  - **No judgement:** Avoid self-criticism or trying to perform perfect movements. The goal is to enjoy the process of dancing and expressing yourself, not to achieve a specific outcome.
- **Cool down:** Gradually slow your movements and take a few moments to stretch or relax your body. Let your breathing return to a normal pace.

- **Journal reflection:** After dancing, take a few moments to write down your thoughts and feelings about the experience. How did it feel to dance freely without choreography? What emotions or sensations did you experience during the dance? How did the music influence your movement and mood? Did you notice any new ways of moving or expressing yourself?

Alternative activities:
- **Dance with a partner:** Invite a friend or family member to join you for a duet freestyle dance session. Enjoy the spontaneous movement together and feed off each other's energy.
- **Soul dance**: Set aside time to play music that inspires you. Move freely and intuitively, allowing your body to express emotions without judgment. Embrace this liberating experience as a form of self-discovery and connection to your inner self.

Reflection:
- How did dancing without choreography affect your enjoyment and freedom of movement?
- What new ways of self-expression did you discover through freestyle dancing?
- How can you integrate more spontaneous dance into your routine to enhance your sense of joy and body awareness?

Origami: Crafting and communicating

Origami, the ancient Japanese art of paper folding, is a creative expression tool that promotes relaxation and mindfulness. Its intricate and meditative processes enhance focus and engage individuals in activities that foster flow experiences, leading to improved emotional regulation and presence. Engaging in origami can result in significant reductions in stress and anxiety, improved mood, and increased feelings of relaxation. By encouraging creativity and mindful engagement, origami serves as a valuable practice for enhancing overall well-being.

Time: 30-45 minutes

Location: At a table or workspace with good lighting

You will need:
- Old newspapers or any scrap paper
- Scissors, for cutting newspaper into squares
- A pen or marker
- A ruler for measuring and cutting
- Decorative items like stickers or coloured pens for additional decoration (optional)

You will learn:
- Basic folding techniques to create simple origami shapes.
- How to combine craft with personal messages.
- The art of mindfulness through hands-on creation and thoughtful communication.

Activity instructions:
- **Prepare your materials:** Arrange your workspace with newspapers, scissors, and other materials. If needed, cut the newspaper into squares. Standard origami paper

is usually 6x6 inches, but you can use any size that feels comfortable for you.

- **Select a simple origami design:** Choose a basic origami project to start with, such as a crane, boat, or paper heart. You can find simple instructions online. Here are a few easy designs:
  - Origami crane: Symbol of peace and hope.
  - Origami boat: Represents journeys and exploration.
  - Origami heart: Expresses love and care.

  Use online tutorials or printed guides to follow step-by-step instructions for creating your chosen origami design.

- **Craft your message:** Once you've completed your origami piece, use a pen or marker to write a personal message on it. This could be a note of encouragement, a wish, a favourite quote, or a heartfelt sentiment. Add any additional decorations, such as stickers or drawings, to enhance your origami piece and make it more meaningful.

- **Share your origami:** If you're comfortable, share your origami with someone special. You could give it as a gift or simply show it to a friend or family member. You might also consider leaving it in a public place for someone to find, along with your message.

Alternative activities:

- **Origami storytelling:** Create origami figures that represent characters or elements from a favourite story. As you fold, narrate the story aloud, connecting the art of origami with storytelling to enhance creativity and imagination.

- **Origami awareness campaign**: Create origami models representing a social issue (e.g., peace cranes for anti-violence). Distribute them in your community to raise awareness, spark conversations, and inspire collective action toward positive change.

Reflection:
- How did making origami and writing messages impact your experience of creativity and mindfulness?
- How did the personal message you wrote enhance the meaning of your origami piece?
- How did sharing or displaying your origami affect your sense of connection with others or your environment?

Recipe adventure: Creative cooking

Cooking is a powerful tool for fostering well-being, promoting creativity, mindfulness, and self-expression. The act of preparing food can significantly reduce stress, elevate mood, and provide a sense of accomplishment. Additionally, cooking for others strengthens social bonds and enhances feelings of connection and gratitude. Engaging in cooking as a creative outlet encourages positive attitudes and provides valuable social opportunities, leading to improved mood and personal acceptance. Overall, cooking not only enhances individual well-being but also enriches social interactions and fosters a greater sense of community.

Time: 30-60 minutes
Location: Your kitchen
You will need:
- Ingredients available in your kitchen
- Basic kitchen tools (e.g., pots, pans, utensils, stove, or oven)

You will learn:
- How to use available ingredients to create a fun and unique dish.
- Techniques for infusing play and imagination into the cooking process.
- The enjoyment of experimenting and tasting a new, homemade meal.

Activity instructions:
- **Gather ingredients:** See what ingredients you have on hand. Consider using a mix of vegetables, grains, proteins, and spices. Arrange your ingredients and

kitchen tools in a way that feels fun and inviting. Create a mini cooking "stage" where you feel inspired to experiment.

- **Create your dish with a playful twist**
    - o **Invent a fun concept:** Think of a playful theme for your dish. For example, you could make "rainbow stir-fry" using colourful vegetables or "mystery soup" where you add a surprise ingredient.
    - o **Mix and match:** Combine ingredients in unexpected ways. Let your imagination guide you – try mixing flavours or textures you wouldn't normally combine. For example, add a hint of sweetness to a savoury dish or mix unusual spices.
    - o **Interactive cooking:** Invite family members or housemates to join in on the fun. Let everyone contribute an ingredient or add their own creative touch to the dish.
- **Cook and experiment:** Cook according to your playful plan. Feel free to improvise and adjust as you go along. Experiment with cooking techniques like sautéing, roasting, or boiling in creative ways.
- **Taste and adjust:** Taste your dish as you cook and make adjustments based on flavour. Have fun with the seasoning – try different spice combinations or add a touch of something unexpected.
- **Serve and enjoy:** Plate your dish and enjoy the meal you've created. Appreciate the flavours and textures and celebrate the creativity that went into it.

Alternative activities:

- **Seasonal ingredient challenge**: Choose seasonal ingredients and create a meal using only those items. This encourages creativity, reduces waste, and enhances awareness of local produce, fostering a deeper connection to the food you prepare.
- **Storytelling dinner**: Invite strangers for a meal focused on storytelling. Each guest shares a personal story related to the food they're serving, creating a meaningful connection and a deeper understanding of each other's backgrounds and experiences.

Reflection:

- How did incorporating playfulness into cooking affect your enjoyment and creativity in the kitchen?
- What did you discover about combining ingredients in new and fun ways?
- How did this playful approach to cooking impact your confidence and willingness to experiment in the kitchen?

Drawing: Visualizing optimum well-being

Drawing enhances well-being by fostering creativity, self-expression, and awareness. The act of drawing significantly reduces stress, improves focus, and facilitates a flow state, promoting deeper engagement in the moment. Furthermore, drawing serves as a healthy outlet for emotional regulation, enabling individuals to process thoughts and feelings effectively. As a form of art therapy, it provides valuable tools for exploring and expressing complex emotions, contributing to overall mental health and resilience. By creating a safe space for individuals to articulate their inner experiences, drawing not only nurtures personal insight but also strengthens coping mechanisms, ultimately enhancing emotional well-being.

Time: 45-60 minutes
Location: Any quiet space with a comfortable setting
You will need:
- Drawing paper, sketchbooks, canvas, pencils, coloured pencils, markers, paints, or any preferred art materials
- Inspirational images, magazines for collages, or digital tools for digital art (optional)

You will learn:
- How to understand and visualise personal ideals of well-being.
- How to use art to explore and express your vision of optimal well-being.
- How creative processes can facilitate self-awareness and mindfulness.

Activity instructions:

- **Define your well-being:** Take a few minutes to reflect on what optimum well-being means to you. Consider aspects such as physical health, mental clarity, emotional balance, relationships, and personal fulfilment. Write a brief description or make a list of qualities, activities, and environments that represent your ideal state of well-being. This can help clarify your vision before you start creating.
- **Prepare your art space:** Arrange your art supplies in a comfortable and well-lit area where you can work uninterrupted. Gather any inspirational images or references if needed.
- **Draw or paint your ideal self:** Using your chosen art medium, begin to create a visual representation of your optimum well-being. This might include:
  - **Scenes or environments:** Depict places or situations where you feel your best, like a peaceful nature scene or a vibrant social setting.
  - **Symbols or icons:** Incorporate symbols that represent different aspects of well-being, such as a heart for emotional health or a sun for positivity.
  - **Self-image:** Draw or paint yourself engaged in activities that signify your highest state of well-being.

  Allow yourself to be free with your creativity. There is no right or wrong way to represent your ideal state of well-being; focus on what feels right to you.
- **Reflect on your artwork:** Take a step back and review your artwork. Reflect on how the elements you included represent your vision of well-being. Write a few sentences about your artwork. What do the different

elements symbolize? How does the piece reflect your personal ideals and goals for well-being?

- **Feedback and insights:** If you're comfortable, share your artwork with a friend, family member, or group. Discuss what you've created and how it represents your vision of optimum well-being. Listen to others' feedback and insights and reflect on any new perspectives they might offer.

Alternative activities:

- **Mindful colouring**: Use adult colouring books or print designs to colour mindfully. Focus on the colours and patterns, allowing creativity to flow while promoting relaxation and a sense of accomplishment through art.
- **Self-portrait reflection**: Create a self-portrait that reflects your current self and another that represents your ideal self. This contrasting exercise enhances self-awareness and highlights personal growth areas, fostering a deeper understanding of your journey.

Reflection:

- How did the process of drawing or painting your ideal self-influence your understanding of well-being?
- What did you learn about yourself through this creative activity?
- How can you use this visual representation to guide your actions and decisions towards achieving your optimum well-being?

Art of photography: Capturing emotions

Photography contributes to a sense of wholeness by encouraging appreciation of the present moment. It allows individuals to capture and reflect on beauty, fostering gratitude and deeper connections with their surroundings. The practice of taking and sharing one photo every day has become a popular way to enhance well-being. This simple activity allows individuals to capture beauty, reflect on positive experiences, and weave new interest into their routines. Studies show that such practices enhance gratitude and expand social relationships, as participants share aesthetically pleasing images and offer positive comments. Additionally, photography promotes self-expression and emotional healing, helping individuals feel more integrated and fulfilled.

Time: 60-75 minutes

Location: Any space where you can observe and photograph a range of emotional expressions and scenes (e.g., home, outdoor settings, community spaces)

You will need:
- Camera or smartphone
- Tripod, lens filters, or photography accessories (optional)
- Photo editing software or apps for post-processing (optional)

You will learn:
- How to capture and express a wide range of emotions through photography.
- How to use photography to visually represent complex emotional states.

- How to explore and reflect on the role of various emotions in the experience of being whole.

Activity instructions:
- **Understand emotional wholeness:** Take a few moments to think about what being whole means to you, including the full range of emotions – joy, sadness, anger, peace, etc. Write down or list different emotions you want to capture. Consider how these emotions contribute to the sense of wholeness.
- **Create an emotional photo list:** Based on your reflections, make a list of scenes or subjects that represent different emotions. For example, "a moment of laughter" for joy, "a quiet, solitary space" for contemplation, or "a dramatic storm" for intensity. Think about how to visually represent each emotion and where you might find or create these scenes.
- **Capture emotional scenes:** Start taking photos based on your list, aiming to capture scenes or moments that embody each identified emotion.
  - **Emotion in people:** Photograph people expressing various emotions, if possible. Look for genuine moments of sadness, joy, anger, or serenity.
  - **Emotion in environment:** Capture elements in your environment that convey emotions. For example, a rain-soaked street might represent melancholy, while a vibrant market scene could show exuberance.

  Experiment with lighting, composition, and focus to enhance the emotional impact of your photos.
- **Assemble your gallery:** Review your images and select the ones that best represent each emotion. Use editing

tools to adjust colours, contrast, and other elements to better convey the intended emotional tone. Arrange your photos in a sequence or layout that reflects the full spectrum of emotions and the concept of wholeness. You can use a digital slideshow or a physical display.
- **Share your captures:** Take time to view your assembled gallery. Reflect on how each image contributes to the theme of emotional wholeness. If you're comfortable, share your gallery with others and discuss the emotions represented. Reflect on their reactions and insights about your depiction of wholeness.

Alternative Activities:
- **Visual poetry:** Create a photo series that expresses a specific emotion through imagery. Pair each photo with a short poem or quote that encapsulates the feeling, blending visual art with literary expression for deeper reflection.
- **Themed projects:** Explore different themes related to emotional depth, such as "the complexity of happiness" or "finding peace amidst chaos."

Reflection:
- How did capturing a range of emotions enhance your understanding of what it means to be whole?
- What did you learn about your own emotional experiences and their role in your sense of completeness?
- How can you continue to use photography to explore and express complex emotional states in your daily life?

Handmade textile: Crafting a personalized gift

Giving handmade gifts fosters meaningful connections by expressing thoughtfulness and care, enhancing gratitude and appreciation. These gifts often carry personal significance, promoting emotional bonds and joy for both giver and receiver, contributing to overall well-being. Textile crafts enhance psychological well-being by fulfilling intrinsic needs related to doing, belonging, becoming, and being. Crafting improves well-being by focusing on creating a purposeful life, achieving self-actualization, fostering social connections, promoting self-empowerment, and providing stress relief.

Time: 3-5 hours (can be spread over multiple sessions)
Location: Your home or a crafting space
You will need:
- Fabric (cotton, linen, or canvas), fabric paints or dyes, embroidery threads, fabric markers, or sewing materials
- Scissors, fabric glue, sewing needle and thread (if sewing), paintbrushes, and an iron
- Sketchbook or paper for design planning, pencils, and erasers
- A gift box, wrapping paper, and decorative items like ribbons or tags

You will learn:
- Techniques for creating handmade textile art, including painting, embroidery, or sewing.
- How to design and craft a textile piece that reflects personal meaning and is tailored to the recipient.
- Basic textile arts skills include painting on fabric, stitching, or assembling textile components.

- **Choose your art form:** Decide on the type of textile art you want to create, such as a painted fabric canvas, embroidered piece, or a sewn item like a tote bag or cushion cover.
- **Design your piece:** Think about the recipient's preferences and interests. Design a piece that reflects their personality or has special meaning. Sketch your design on paper. Choose the appropriate fabric and art supplies based on your design. For painting, you'll need fabric paints; for embroidery, you'll need threads and needles.
- **Prepare the fabric**
  - **For painting:** Wash and iron the fabric to remove any wrinkles or residues. Lay it flat on a surface protected by a newspaper or a craft mat.
  - **For embroidery or sewing:** Cut and prepare the fabric to the required size and shape for your project.
- **Execute the design**
  - **Painting:** Use fabric paints and brushes to apply your design to the fabric. Allow each layer to dry completely before applying additional layers.
  - **Embroidery:** Transfer your design onto the fabric using a fabric marker. Stitch your design using embroidery threads and various stitches.
  - **Sewing:** If creating a sewn item, cut the fabric pieces according to your design and sew them together. Add any additional elements like pockets or appliqués.

- **Finishing touches**
  - **For painted fabrics:** Set the paint by ironing the fabric on the reverse side according to the instructions.
  - **For embroidered or sewn items:** Trim loose threads and secure all seams.
- **Gift wrapping**
  - **Wrap your art:** Fold or roll the textile art neatly, place it in a gift box, or wrap it in decorative paper.
  - **Add a personal touch:** Attach a ribbon or gift tag. You might include a handwritten note explaining the significance of the art or expressing your thoughts for the recipient.
- **Gift giving:** Arrange a time to present the gift to the recipient. You might choose to give it in person or send it through the mail with a personal message.

Alternative activities:
- **Personalized keychains:** Make fabric keychains by sewing small fabric squares or shapes. Personalize them with initials or symbols that reflect the recipient's personality, making for a functional yet meaningful gift.
- **Fabric bookmarks:** Create personalized fabric bookmarks by sewing together different fabrics and embellishing with embroidery or fabric paint. These thoughtful gifts add a personal touch to any book lover's collection.

Reflection:
- How did creating handmade textile art enhance your appreciation for textile arts and crafting?
- How did personalising the art for someone special impact your experience and the final piece?
- How can you use these skills in crafting projects or gifts?

Videomaking: Personal life journey

Videomaking fosters creativity, self-expression, and storytelling, allowing individuals to process experiences and emotions. It encourages collaboration and connection with others, enhancing social bonds. Studies have shown that engaging in video creation can boost confidence, provide a sense of accomplishment, and promote mindfulness, contributing to overall well-being. Furthermore, videomaking facilitates deeper engagement with subjects, enhances critical thinking skills, and encourages dynamic representations of concepts, ultimately enriching the educational experience and personal growth.

Time: 90-120 minutes

Location: Any space where you can film and gather visual content

You will need:
- Smartphone or camera
- Instagram's built-in editor, or other video editing apps like InShot
- Personal photos, old videos, or visual content that represents significant moments in your life
- Items or settings that are meaningful to you and help illustrate your story

You will learn:
- How to craft and present a personal narrative through video.
- Basic skills in filming and editing for storytelling.
- How to explore and share key moments and milestones in your life.

Activity instructions:

- **Reflect on your life journey:** Think about significant events, achievements, challenges, and milestones in your life. Consider moments that have shaped who you are today. Make a rough timeline of these key moments. This will help you structure your video and decide what content to include.
- **Plan your video:** Outline the structure of your video. Introduce yourself and provide an overview of what the video will cover. Divide your life journey into segments, such as childhood, important achievements, challenges overcome, and current life. Reflect on your journey and share any final thoughts or future goals. Select background music that complements the tone of your video.
- **Gather photos and videos:** Gather personal photos, old videos, and any visual content that represents key moments in your life. Set up any props or backgrounds that will enhance your video. For instance, use items related to significant milestones or achievements.
- **Film your video:**
  - **Record segments:** Film yourself narrating or reflecting on each key moment. Use a mix of direct-to-camera speaking and voiceovers if necessary.
  - **Incorporate visuals:** Integrate your collected photos and videos into your footage. Use these visuals to illustrate the narrative and provide context to your story.
  - **Be authentic:** Share personal reflections and emotions to create a genuine and engaging narrative.

- **Edit your video:** Use editing software to arrange your footage and visuals according to your storyboard. Trim and adjust clips for a smooth flow. Include text overlays for names, dates, or key points. Use transitions and effects to enhance the storytelling. Add your chosen background music and adjust the volume to ensure it complements your narration.
- **Preview and share:** Watch the final version to ensure it tells your story clearly and effectively. Make any necessary adjustments. Upload your video to a platform of your choice, such as YouTube, Instagram, or a personal blog.

Alternative activities:
- **Wellness interviews:** Film interviews with local wellness practitioners, such as yoga instructors or therapists, discussing their practices and insights. This activity promotes community connection while providing valuable resources for viewers interested in improving their well-being.
- **Create vlogs**: Create a series of vlogs documenting your personal wellness journey, including practices like meditation, exercise, or nutrition. Share insights, challenges, and triumphs to inspire others while fostering your self-reflection and growth.

Reflection:
- How did creating this video help you reflect on and express your life journey?
- What impact do you hope your video will have on yourself and others who view it?
- How can you use video to explore and share other aspects of your life or experiences?

Herb corner: Garden with personalized pots

Gardening enhances well-being by promoting relaxation, awareness, and a deep connection with nature. Research indicates that introducing houseplants can lead to significant decreases in perceived stress and healthier cortisol patterns, suggesting improved health status. Additionally, gardening can help combat loneliness by fostering social interactions and community engagement. Individuals often report socio-cultural benefits from gardening, including enhanced relaxation, increased positive emotions, and a greater sense of pride in their surroundings. Research findings highlight the importance of residential gardens in contributing to stress management, social connectedness, and overall well-being, particularly in urban environments where access to green spaces is limited.

Time: 45-60 minutes
Location: Garden, balcony, or any outdoor space suitable for planting
You will need:
- Indian herbs such as mint, coriander, tulsi, curry leaves, or fenugreek
- Potting soil and containers
- Basic tools like trowels, gloves, and watering cans
- Paints, brushes, and markers for decorating pots, stones, driftwood, or plant markers

You will learn:
- Creative planting and arranging of Indian herbs.
- Building a deeper bond with nature through cultivating useful plants.

- How gardening and personalizing pots can enhance the meditative experience.

Activity instructions:
- **Plan your herbal garden:** Select Indian herbs you want to grow. Sketch out a design for your herb garden, including how you'll arrange the herbs and the decorations.
- **Prepare your planting space:** Choose where to plant your herbs. Fill containers with potting soil or ensure garden beds are ready for planting.
- **Personalize your pots:**
  - **Paint your pots:** Use paints to decorate your pots with colours or designs that inspire you. Allow them to dry before planting.
  - **Name your pots:** Write or paint the names of the herbs on the pots. This can be a fun and creative way to keep track of your plants and add a personal touch.
- **Plant and arrange:** Plant your selected herbs according to your design. Arrange them based on height, colour, and texture. Enhance your garden with additional decorative items like small stones.
- **Ongoing care:** Appreciate the personal touches you added and how they contribute to the overall design of your garden. Water your herbs as needed and monitor their growth. Adjust your garden design as necessary.

Alternative activities:
- **Seed bombs**: Create seed bombs by mixing native wildflower seeds with clay and compost. Shape them into small balls and toss them in neglected areas,

contributing to local biodiversity while enjoying a creative gardening activity.
- **Compost creation**: Begin a simple compost bin using kitchen scraps (fruit peels, vegetable waste) and yard debris (leaves, grass clippings). This activity teaches sustainability and enriches soil for future gardening projects, benefiting the environment.

Reflection:
- How did personalizing your pots enhance your gardening experience?
- What did you learn about your connection with nature and yourself through this activity?
- How can you continue to infuse creativity into your gardening routine?

Humour: Not taking life too seriously

Humour is a powerful tool for enhancing well-being, promoting laughter, reducing stress, and fostering social connections. It boosts mood and encourages resilience in challenging situations, contributing to overall life satisfaction. Creative writing infused with humour serves as an effective outlet for self-expression and emotional exploration. In one study, participants in a humour program showed significant improvements in emotional well-being, with increased self-efficacy, positive affect, and optimism, along with reduced stress, depression, and anxiety. By incorporating humour into creative writing, individuals can process experiences light-heartedly, fostering resilience and connection with others, making it a valuable resource for enhancing mental and emotional health.

Time: 60-90 minutes
Location: Any comfortable writing space
You will need:
- Notebook or computer
- Pen or keyboard
- Examples of comic poetry, humorous blog posts for reference (optional)

You will learn:
- How to use humour in writing to convey a message about not taking life too seriously.
- Techniques for crafting comic poetry or blog posts.
- How to explore and share a light-hearted perspective on life.

Activity instructions:

- **Choose your format:** Decide whether you want to write a comic poem or blog post. Each format offers a unique way to explore humour:
    - **Comic poetry:** Use rhyme, rhythm, and playful language to create a humorous poem.
    - **Blog post:** Write a funny and engaging post that offers reflections or anecdotes about not taking life too seriously.
- **Brainstorm ideas:** Think about moments when humour helped you deal with life's challenges or how lightening up has made a difference. Consider themes like everyday absurdities, amusing personal anecdotes, or funny observations about human behaviour.
- **Generate content ideas:** Jot down ideas for scenes, characters, or situations that could be depicted in your chosen format. For example:
    - **Comic poem:** Write about a day where everything goes hilariously wrong, but the character finds joy in the chaos.
    - **Blog post:** Share a humorous list of "Top 10 ways to not take life too seriously" based on personal experiences.
- **Draft your piece:** Choose a simple rhyme scheme or free verse. Focus on playful language and rhythm. Write about a humorous situation or a series of funny observations. Use exaggeration and clever wordplay. Begin with an engaging introduction, followed by the main content, and conclude with a light-hearted wrap-up. Incorporate personal anecdotes, funny reflections, or humorous advice. Keep the tone conversational and engaging.

- **Revise for clarity:** Reread your piece to ensure it effectively conveys humour and the theme of lightening up. Make adjustments to improve the flow, timing, and impact of your humour. Include any final touches, such as punchlines, witty remarks, or playful language.
- **Share to spread joy:** If you're comfortable, share your comic poetry or blog post with friends, family, or on social media. Ask for feedback on how effectively your writing conveys the message of not taking life too seriously.

Alternative activities:
- **Comic strip creation:** Create a simple comic strip depicting an exaggerated version of a personal experience or a funny situation. Visual humour helps ease stress, enhancing both creativity and emotional well-being.
- **Meme challenge:** Create memes focused on wellness, using humour to address mental health challenges. This activity encourages dialogue around mental health issues while lightening the mood, fostering both awareness and emotional balance.

Reflection:
- How did writing humorously help you explore the theme of not taking life too seriously?
- What impact do you hope your piece will have on readers and on yourself?
- How can you continue to use humour in your writing to address other themes or experiences?

Slow down with pottery: Handcrafting a cup

Pottery enhances well-being by promoting mindfulness and creativity. The tactile experience of working with clay encourages focus and relaxation, effectively reducing stress. Additionally, pottery fosters a sense of accomplishment and self-expression, helping individuals connect with their emotions while developing patience and resilience. Research indicates that pottery workshops can significantly improve mood and self-esteem. Participants in these workshops often report increased sustained attention and pleasure, along with decreased levels of negative affect and sadness. Overall, engaging in pottery can provide therapeutic benefits, contributing to emotional well-being and psychological health.

Time: 2-3 hours
Location: Pottery studio, kitchen table, or any space with access to pottery materials
You will need:
- Stoneware or earthenware clay suitable for hand-building
- Basic tools such as a rolling pin, knife, sponge, and a rib tool, alternatively, you can use household items like a rolling pin and butter knife
- Water for smoothing and shaping the clay
- Kiln access for firing the pottery (if available), alternatively, use air-dry clay if you don't have kiln access

You will learn:
- How working with clay can be a meditative and calming experience.
- Basic hand-building techniques to create a functional and unique cup.

- How to design and craft a personal item that reflects your individuality and creativity.

Activity instructions:
- **Prepare your workspace:** Arrange your materials and tools on a clean, flat surface. If you're working with a group, ensure everyone has enough space and materials. Cover your workspace with a cloth or plastic to catch any clay spills.
- **Get to know the clay:** Knead the clay to make it pliable and remove any air bubbles. This is called "wedging" and helps prevent cracks during shaping. Take a moment to feel the texture and weight of the clay. Let the sensory experience of the clay help you relax and focus.
- **Create the base:** Roll out a piece of clay into a flat, even slab using a rolling pin. Use a round template (like a small plate) to cut out a circular piece of clay for the bottom of your cup.
- **Build the walls:** Roll out additional clay into long, even strips. These will form the walls of your cup. Wrap the strips around the base, smoothing the edges to blend the pieces together. Use a sponge or your fingers to smooth the joints and create a seamless wall.
- **Shape and refine:** Use your hands or a rib tool to shape and smooth the walls of the cup. Create a slight flare at the top if desired.
- **Add a handle:** Roll a small piece of clay into a coil, shape it into a handle, and attach it to the side of the cup. Smooth the attachment points and ensure it is securely attached.
- **Let it dry:** If you're using air-dry clay, let your cup dry according to the manufacturer's instructions. This

usually takes 24-48 hours. If you have access to a kiln, fire your cup according to the clay type and kiln specifications.
- **Enjoy your creation:** Take a moment to appreciate your handmade cup. Reflect on the process and how it helped you slow down and connect with the material. Use your cup for your favourite beverage or display it as a personal piece of art.

Alternative activities:
- **Bowl of calm**: Create a bowl as a symbol of nurturing. Let each stroke of your hands shape the clay slowly, cultivating a sense of inner peace and practicing mindfulness during the slow, rhythmic motions.
- **Nature-inspired coasters**: Handcraft coasters by pressing dried flowers into clay. This process allows you to connect with nature while creating functional art that brings a touch of serenity to your everyday life.

Reflection:
- How did working with clay help you slow down and connect with the present moment?
- What did you learn about yourself through the process of crafting your cup?
- How can you use pottery or other creative activities to continue cultivating mindfulness and relaxation?

Creative writing: Inspiring poetry or story

Creative writing promotes self-expression, emotional processing, and personal reflection, allowing individuals to explore their thoughts and feelings. This practice enhances self-awareness and clarity, while also reducing stress and boosting mood. Research indicates that creative writing can improve mental well-being. A study of a creative writing group revealed a complex relationship between cathartic expression and the quality of writing produced, with participants experiencing therapeutic benefits. Overall, creative writing serves as a valuable tool for enhancing emotional well-being and enabling a sense of accomplishment.

Time: 90-120 minutes
Location: Any comfortable writing space
You will need:
- Notebook or computer
- Pen or keyboard
- Inspirational materials (optional)

You will learn:
- How to craft written content that inspires and motivates others.
- Techniques for writing poetry or short stories with an inspirational message.
- How to effectively communicate a message that uplifts and encourages readers.

Activity instructions:
- **Define your inspirational message:** Think about what inspires you and how you want to inspire others.

Consider themes such as perseverance, personal growth, kindness, or overcoming challenges.

- **Select your format:** Decide whether you want to write a poem, blog post, or short story. Each format offers a unique way to deliver your message:
    - **Poetry:** Use lyrical language and metaphor to evoke emotion and inspiration.
    - **Short story:** Create a narrative that illustrates inspirational themes through fictional characters and events.
- **Brainstorm and outline:** Think about personal experiences, quotes, or stories that have inspired you. How can these be translated into your chosen format? Create a rough outline for your writing:
    - **Poetry:** Plan the structure, themes, and key imagery. Consider how you will use language to create an emotional impact.
    - **Short story:** Develop a basic plot, including the setup, conflict, and resolution. Create characters and scenarios that will highlight your inspirational message.
- **Write your piece**
    - **Draft your poem:** Write a poem that conveys your inspirational message. Focus on using evocative language, vivid imagery, and emotional resonance. Refine your poem to enhance its emotional and inspirational effect. Pay attention to rhythm, word choice, and overall flow.
    - **Draft your story:** Write the narrative, focusing on how the story illustrates your inspirational message. Develop characters and events that highlight growth, resilience, or positivity

themes. Refine your story to enhance character development, plot, and emotional impact. Ensure the story effectively conveys the inspirational message.

- **Review your writing:** Reread your piece to ensure it effectively communicates your inspirational message. Look for areas that could be improved for clarity and impact. If possible, share your draft with someone you trust for feedback on how well it inspires and engages readers.
- **Encourage interaction:** Publish your poem or short story on a platform of your choice, such as a personal blog, social media, or a community forum. Invite readers to share their thoughts and reflections on your work. Engage with their feedback and respond to comments.

Alternative activities:
- **Empathy poem**: Write a poem that captures the power of empathy and kindness in everyday interactions. Use vivid imagery to inspire readers to connect with others and promote compassion in their lives.
- **Short story of hope**: Craft a short story about a character who overcomes adversity with hope and determination. Through storytelling, inspire readers to find their inner strength and persevere through tough times.

Reflection:
- How did crafting this piece help you express and communicate an inspirational message?

- What impact do you hope your writing will have on readers? How do you want them to feel or think after engaging with your piece?
- How can you continue to use writing to inspire and motivate others in future projects?

Exploration: A farmers market visit

Exploration enhances well-being by fostering curiosity, spontaneity, and personal growth. Engaging in new experiences builds resilience, boosts confidence, and nurtures social connections. Such activities stimulate both the mind and body, leading to increased happiness and fulfilment, while also broadening one's perspective on life. For example, exploring local farmers' markets can foster a strong sense of community by connecting individuals to local producers and their community. The act of purchasing local food not only provides access to fresh products but also creates a psychological bond, reinforcing social ties, promoting shared values, and contributing to a sense of belonging and support within the community.

Time: 2-3 hours
Location: A local farmers market in your area
You will need:
- Comfortable clothing, reusable shopping bags, cash
- Information about the market's location, hours
- Notebook or journal
- Camera or phone

You will learn:
- Insights into local farming practices and seasonal produce.
- Understanding of the variety of fresh, local foods available and their sources.
- How interacting with local vendors and farmers fosters a connection with your community.

Activity instructions:

- **Pre-visit preparation:** Look up the local farmers market to gather information about its location, operating hours, and types of vendors. Identify any special events or activities happening on the day of your visit. Prepare a list of things you'd like to see or try at the market. Make sure to dress comfortably and bring reusable shopping bags and cash.

- **Market walkthrough:** Start by walking through the market to understand its layout and the types of products available. Take note of different sections such as produce, baked goods, and artisan crafts. Visit various stalls and engage with vendors. Ask questions about their products, farming practices, and any seasonal specialities.

- **Taste local products:** Try samples of fresh produce, baked goods, or other local products available at the market. Notice the flavours and ingredients that stand out. Buy a few items that intrigue you, such as fresh fruits, vegetables, or homemade treats. Consider purchasing items you haven't tried before.

- **Learn about local farming:** Talk to vendors about their farming methods and their challenges. Ask about the seasonal cycles and what's unique about their produce. Learn about where the food comes from and any unique growing techniques or sustainable practices they use.

- **Cultural insights:** Observe any traditional or regional practices related to food and farming. Note how these practices are reflected in the market. Notice how the market functions as a community hub and how vendors interact with customers.

- **Document your experience:** Find a spot to sit and write about your experience at the market. Include details about the products you tried, interactions with vendors, and any insights gained. Review and organise your photos, capturing the vibrancy and diversity of the market. Add captions or notes to remember specific moments.

Alternative activities:
- **Meet the beekeepers**: Visit local beekeepers at their stalls. Learn about the importance of bees in agriculture, their role in pollination, and how to support local honey production.
- **Cultural performances**: Enjoy live performances featuring local musicians or dancers at the market. These cultural showcases enrich the market experience and celebrate the diverse talents within the community.

Reflection:
- How did visiting the farmers market enhance your understanding of local agriculture and food systems?
- What did you learn about the community and its relationship with local food through this market visit?
- How can you continue supporting local farmers and markets in your community, and how might this experience influence your food choices?

Cultural day trip: Appreciate diversity

Meaningful travel enhances well-being by fostering personal growth, cultural understanding, and connection with others. It promotes mindfulness and appreciation of diverse experiences, cultivating gratitude and reflection. Cultural exploration broadens perspectives and deepens empathy by exposing individuals to new traditions and beliefs. Travel also boosts hedonic well-being by encouraging engagement in physical and social activities while reducing ruminative thinking and daily obligations. The distance from everyday life offers mental relief, and though travel's benefits may be similar to time spent at home, its sense of novelty and remoteness creates lasting memories, self-awareness, and purpose.

Time: 6-8 hours

Location: A nearby city or town with a distinct cultural community or heritage

You will need:

- Maps, transportation (car or public transit), a basic itinerary
- Information on cultural sites, events, and local attractions
- Notebook or journal
- Camera or phone

You will learn:

- How engaging with a different cultural community can enhance your understanding and appreciation of diversity.
- Insights into a different cultural group's daily lives, traditions, and customs.

- How interacting with and observing cultural differences can broaden your perspective.

Activity instructions:
- **Pre-trip preparation:** Choose a nearby city or neighbourhood known for its cultural diversity or historical significance. Research the area to identify key cultural sites, events, and restaurants. Plan a route that includes visits to cultural landmarks, local eateries, and community events. Ensure that you have time allocated for each activity.
- **Morning cultural exploration:** Start your day by visiting a cultural landmark such as a museum, historical site, or cultural centre. Take a guided tour, if available, to gain deeper insights. Capture photos and take notes on the history and significance of the site.
- **Traditional meal:** Head to a local restaurant or market that features traditional cuisine from the culture you're exploring. Try a few dishes and pay attention to the ingredients and flavours. Take a moment to reflect on the culinary experience. Note any new flavours or dining customs.
- **Afternoon immersion and interaction:** Interact with community members to learn more about their customs and daily life. Visit a local market or shopping district to explore traditional crafts, clothing, and products. Observe how these items reflect the local culture.
- **Late afternoon events:** Check for local cultural events, festivals, or performances during your visit. Attend one to experience traditional music, dance, or arts.
- **Reflection and integration:** Find a quiet spot to sit and write a journal entry about your day. Reflect on what you learned about the culture, how it affected

your understanding of diversity, and any personal insights gained. Review and organise your photos. Add captions or notes to remember specific moments.
- **Social sharing and discussion:** If you're with others, discuss your experiences and reflections. Share what you found most interesting or impactful. Create a brief summary or photo collage to share on social media, highlighting the cultural aspects you explored.

Alternative activities:
- **Cultural workshop:** Attend a short workshop or class that offers a hands-on experience with a traditional craft or art form from the culture.
- **Community festivals:** Attend local cultural festivals to experience traditional music, dance, and food. Immerse yourself in the vibrant atmosphere while connecting with community members and appreciating diverse cultural expressions.

Reflection:
- How did the day trip help you better understand and appreciate the area's cultural diversity?
- What new perspectives or insights did you gain from interacting with and observing a different culture?
- How can you apply this experience to further explore and appreciate other cultures in your daily life or future travels?

Conclusion: Journey continues!

As you reach the end of this book, I hope you feel a renewed sense of connection to yourself, others, and the world around you. Well-being is not a destination, but an ongoing journey – one that requires continual nurturing, reflection, and adaptation. Through the science of well-being, your connection to nature, spiritual practices, and creative expression, you now have a diverse toolkit to draw from, no matter where you are in life.

Reflecting on the journey

Take a moment to reflect on the practices and activities you've explored. What resonated most with you? Which practices felt challenging, and why? Well-being is personal, and your journey through it will evolve over time. The important thing is not perfection, but the intention to keep moving forward, with compassion and curiosity.

Integrating well-being into everyday life

The real magic happens in small moments of everyday life. Whether it's pausing to appreciate a beautiful sunset, practicing mindful breathing, or expressing gratitude, well-being interventions can be woven into the fabric of your everyday life. As you move forward, consider these guiding principles for sustaining your practice:

- **Stay present:** Life is constantly changing, and so will your well-being needs. Stay present with your experiences, and regularly check in with yourself to see how your mind, body, and spirit are doing.
- **Create rituals:** Establish simple, daily rituals that anchor your well-being practice. These could be

morning stretches, evening gratitude reflections, or a nature walk post dinner. Consistency is key, and even the smallest efforts can have profound effects over time.

- **Be flexible:** Life can be unpredictable. Allow yourself the flexibility to adapt your practices based on your current circumstances. Some days, a quick meditation or creative exercise might be enough, while other times, you may feel drawn to deeper practices like extended time in nature or a silence retreat.
- **Reflect and adjust:** Periodically reflect on your progress and how the practices are influencing your life. Are you feeling more grounded? More energized? If something doesn't feel aligned anymore, adjust the practice or try something new. This is your personal journey, and it's important to stay attuned to what serves you best.
- **Find community:** While well-being is a deeply personal journey, it can also be enhanced by sharing it with others. Consider finding a community that aligns with your well-being goals, whether through yoga classes, nature groups, or creative workshops. Engaging with like-minded people can provide support, accountability, and fresh perspectives.

Reaching out for support

While this book offers tools and insights for nurturing your well-being, it's essential to recognize that there may be times when you encounter mental health challenges that require additional support. If you find yourself feeling overwhelmed, persistently sad, anxious, or struggling to cope, please consider reaching out to a mental health professional. Seeking help is a courageous step and an important part of your journey toward well-being.

Mental health professionals, including therapists, counsellors, and psychiatrists, are equipped to provide support, guidance, and interventions tailored to your unique needs. Just as you would consult a doctor for a physical ailment, prioritizing your mental health is vital for overall well-being. Remember, you don't have to navigate this journey alone. Support is available, and it's okay to ask for it.

Continuing the practice

Well-being is not something you master in a few weeks or months. It's a lifelong practice, evolving as you evolve. The micro interventions you've gained here – whether through positive psychology, nature connectedness, spirituality, or creativity – are meant to be revisited, reimagined, and integrated into the rhythm of your life.

Remember, there's no right or wrong way to practice these well-being interventions. It's about staying open, curious, and kind to yourself as you navigate life's ups and downs. Let this book serve as a guide you can return to whenever you need inspiration, comfort, or a reminder of what truly matters.

Your next chapter

As you close this book, a new chapter in your mental health and well-being journey begins. Trust that the practices you've learned are here to support you, and that you have the wisdom within to continue growing and flourishing. With each step forward, embrace the small, mindful moments that bring joy, peace, and connection into your life.

Thank you for taking this journey with me. May you continue to be well and craft a meaningful life for sustained happiness.

Resources

Section 1: Positive Psychology Interventions

1. Seligman, M. E., & Csikszentmihalyi, M. (2000). Positive psychology: An introduction. *American Psychologist, 55*(1), 5-14. https://doi.org/10.1037/0003-066X.55.1.5

2. Seligman, M. (2018). PERMA and the building blocks of well-being. *The Journal of Positive Psychology, 13*(4), 333-335. https://doi.org/10.1080/17439760.2018.1437466

3. Carr, A., Cullen, K., Keeney, C., Canning, C., Mooney, O., Chinseallaigh, E., & O'Dowd, A. (2021). Effectiveness of positive psychology interventions: A systematic review and meta-analysis. *The Journal of Positive Psychology, 16*(6), 749-769. https://doi.org/10.1080/17439760.2020.1818807

4. Emmons, R. A., Froh, J., & Rose, R. (2019). Gratitude. In M. W. Gallagher & S. J. Lopez (Eds.), *Positive psychological assessment: A handbook of models and measures* (2nd ed., pp. 317–332). American Psychological Association. https://doi.org/10.1037/0000138-020

5. Rash, J. A., Matsuba, M. K., & Prkachin, K. M. (2011). Gratitude and well-being: Who benefits the most from a gratitude intervention? *Applied Psychology: Health and Well-Being, 3*(3), 350-369. https://doi.org/10.1111/j.1758-0854.2011.01058.x

6. Bryant, F. (2003). Savoring Beliefs Inventory (SBI): A scale for measuring beliefs about savoring. *Journal of Mental Health, 12*(2), 175–196. https://doi.org/10.1080/0963823031000103489

7. Samios, C., Catania, J., Newton, K., Fulton, T., & Breadman, A. (2020). Stress, savoring, and coping: The role of savoring in psychological adjustment following a stressful life event. *Stress and Health, 36*(2), 119-130. https://doi.org/10.1002/smi.2914

8. Engeser, S., Schiepe-Tiska, A., & Peifer, C. (2021). Historical lines and an overview of current research on flow. In S. Engeser & A. Schiepe-Tiska (Eds.), *Advances in flow research* (pp. 1-29). Springer. https://doi.org/10.1007/978-3-030-53468-4_1

9. Park, N., & Peterson, C. (2009). Character strengths: Research and practice. *Journal of College and Character, 10*(4), 1-10. https://doi.org/10.2202/1940-1639.1042

10. Fredrickson, B. L. (2001). The role of positive emotions in positive psychology: The broaden-and-build theory of positive emotions. *American Psychologist, 56*(3), 218–226. https://doi.org/10.1037/0003-066X.56.3.218

11. Fredrickson, B. L., Cohn, M. A., Coffey, K. A., Pek, J., & Finkel, S. M. (2008). Open hearts build lives: Positive emotions, induced through loving-kindness meditation, build consequential personal resources. *Journal of Personality and Social Psychology, 95*(5), 1045-1062. https://doi.org/10.1037/a0013262

12. Kiken, L. G., & Shook, N. J. (2011). Looking up: Mindfulness increases positive judgments and reduces negativity bias. *Social Psychological and Personality Science, 2*(4), 425-431. https://doi.org/10.1177/1948550610396585

13. Woods, S., Lambert, N., Brown, P., Fincham, F., & May, R. (2015). "I'm so excited for you!" How an enthusiastic responding intervention enhances close relationships. *Journal of Social and Personal Relationships, 32*(1), 24-40. https://doi.org/10.1177/0265407514523545

14. Carver, C. S., & Scheier, M. F. (2014). Dispositional optimism. *Trends in Cognitive Sciences, 18*(6), 293-299. https://doi.org/10.1016/j.tics.2014.02.003

15. Littman-Ovadia, H., & Nir, D. (2013). Looking forward to tomorrow: The buffering effect of a daily optimism intervention. *The Journal of Positive Psychology, 9*(2), 122–136. https://doi.org/10.1080/17439760.2013.853202

16. Neff, K. D. (2011). Self-compassion, self-esteem, and well-being. *Social and Personality Psychology Compass, 5*(1), 1-12. https://doi.org/10.1111/j.1751-9004.2010.00330.x

17. Wilson, J. M., Weiss, A., & Shook, N. J. (2020). Mindfulness, self-compassion, and savoring: Factors that explain the relation between perceived social support and well-being. *Personality and Individual Differences, 152*, 109568. https://doi.org/10.1016/j.paid.2019.109568

18. Engeser, S., Schiepe-Tiska, A., & Peifer, C. (2021). Historical lines and an overview of current research on flow. In S. Engeser & A. Schiepe-Tiska (Eds.), *Advances in flow research* (pp. 1-29). Springer. https://doi.org/10.1007/978-3-030-53468-4_1

19. Stamatelopoulou, F., Pezirkianidis, C., Karakasidou, E., Lakioti, A., & Stalikas, A. (2018). "Being in the zone": A systematic review on the relationship of

psychological correlates and the occurrence of flow experiences in sports' performance. *Psychology, 9*(8), 2011-2032. https://doi.org/10.4236/psych.2018.98115

20. Schippers, M. C., & Hogenes, R. (2011). Energy management of people in organizations: A review and research agenda. *Journal of Business and Psychology, 26*(2), 193-203. https://doi.org/10.1007/s10869-011-9217-6

21. Schwartz, T., & McCarthy, C. (2007). Manage your energy, not your time. *Harvard Business Review, 85*(10), 63-73. https://hbr.org/2007/10/manage-your-energy-not-your-time

22. Dweck, C. (2016). What having a "growth mindset" actually means. *Harvard Business Review, 13*(2), 2-5. https://hbr.org/2016/01/what-having-a-growth-mindset-actually-means

23. Zhao, S., Du, H., Li, Q., Wu, Q., & Chi, P. (2021). Growth mindset of socioeconomic status boosts subjective well-being: A longitudinal study. *Personality and Individual Differences, 168*, 110301. https://doi.org/10.1016/j.paid.2020.110301

24. Herrman, H., Stewart, D. E., Diaz-Granados, N., Berger, E. L., Jackson, B., & Yuen, T. (2011). What is resilience? *The Canadian Journal of Psychiatry, 56*(5), 258-265. https://doi.org/10.1177/070674371105600504

25. Mayordomo, T., Viguer, P., Sales, A., Satorres, E., & Meléndez, J. C. (2021). Resilience and coping as predictors of well-being in adults. In *Mental health and psychopathology* (pp. 265-277). Routledge. https://doi.org/10.1080/00223980.2016.1203276

26. Lunenburg, F. C. (2011). Goal-setting theory of motivation. *International Journal of Management,*

Business, and Administration, 15(1), 1-6. https://static1. squarespace.com/static/5b0b8f55365f02045e1ecaa5/ t/5b14d215758d46f9851858d1/1528091160453/ Lunenburg%2C+Fred+C.+Goal-Setting+Theoryof+ Motivation+IJMBA+V15+N1+2011.pdf

27. Seijts, G. H., & Latham, G. P. (2012). Knowing when to set learning versus performance goals. *Organizational Dynamics, 41*(1), 1-6. http://dx.doi.org/10.1016/j. orgdyn.2011.12.001

28. Newman, G. E. (2019). The psychology of authenticity. *Review of General Psychology, 23*(1), 8-18. https://doi.org/10.1037/gpr0000158

29. Kipfelsberger, P., Braun, S., Fladerer, M. P., & Dragoni, L. (2022). Developing authenticity: A quasi-experimental investigation. *Personality and Individual Differences, 198*, 111825. https://doi.org/10.1016/j. paid.2022.111825

30. Kaya, M., & Erdem, C. (2021). Students' well-being and academic achievement: A meta-analysis study. *Child Indicators Research, 14*(5), 1743–1767. https://doi.org/10.1007/s12187-021-09821-4

Section 2: Nature-based Interventions

1. Ulrich, R. S. (2023). Stress reduction theory. In D. Marchand, E. Pol, & K. Weiss (Eds.), *Stress reduction theory* (pp. 143-146). https://www.researchgate.net/ publication/377281012_Ulrich_RS_2023_Stress_ reduction_theory

2. Basu, A., Duvall, J., & Kaplan, R. (2019). Attention restoration theory: Exploring the role of soft fascination and mental bandwidth. *Environment and Behavior, 51*(9-10), 1055-1081. https://doi. org/10.1177/0013916518774400

3. Pritchard, A., Richardson, M., Sheffield, D., & McEwan, K. (2020). The relationship between nature connectedness and eudaimonic well-being: A meta-analysis. *Journal of Happiness Studies, 21*, 1145-1167. https://doi.org/10.1007/s10902-019-00118-6

4. Lumber, R., Richardson, M., & Sheffield, D. (2017). Beyond knowing nature: Contact, emotion, compassion, meaning, and beauty are pathways to nature connection. *PLOS One, 12*(5), e0177186. https://doi.org/10.1371/journal.pone.0177186

5. Sheffield, D., Butler, C. W., & Richardson, M. (2022). Improving nature connectedness in adults: A meta-analysis, review, and agenda. *Sustainability, 14*(19), 12494. https://doi.org/10.3390/su141912494

6. Lahoti, S. A., Dhyani, S., Sahle, M., Kumar, P., & Saito, O. (2024). Exploring the nexus between green space availability, connection with nature, and pro-environmental behavior in the urban landscape. *Sustainability, 16*(13), 5435. https://doi.org/10.3390/su16135435

7. Gola, M., Botta, M., D'Aniello, A. L., & Capolongo, S. (2022). How breaks in nature can affect the users' well-being: An experience-based survey during the lockdown. *European Journal of Public Health, 32*(Supplement_3), ckac129-708. https://doi.org/10.1093/eurpub/ckac129.708

8. de Bloom, J., Kinnunen, U., & Korpela, K. (2014). Exposure to nature versus relaxation during lunch breaks and recovery from work: Development and design of an intervention study to improve workers' health, well-being, work performance, and creativity. *BMC Public Health, 14*(488). https://doi.org/10.1186/1471-2458-14-488

9. Buckley, R. (2023). Birdsong and mental health. *Journal of Environmental Psychology*. https://psycnet.apa.org/doi/10.1016/j.jenvp.2023.102002

10. Passmore, H. A., & Holder, M. D. (2016). Noticing nature: Individual and social benefits of a two-week intervention. *The Journal of Positive Psychology, 12*(6), 537–546. https://doi.org/10.1080/17439760.2016.1221126

11. Løvoll, H. S., Sæther, K. W., & Graves, M. (2020). Feeling at home in the wilderness: Environmental conditions, well-being, and aesthetic experience. *Frontiers in Psychology, 11*, 402. https://doi.org/10.3389/fpsyg.2020.00402

12. Bell, R., Irvine, K. N., Wilson, C., & Warber, S. L. (2014). Dark nature: Exploring potential benefits of nocturnal nature-based interaction for human and environmental health. *European Journal of Ecopsychology, 5*(1), 1-15. https://www.researchgate.net/publication/305041212_Dark_Nature_Exploring_potential_benefits_of_nocturnal_nature-based_interaction_for_human_and_environmental_health

13. Barnes, C., & Passmore, H. A. (2024). Development and testing of the Night Sky Connectedness Index (NSCI). *Journal of Environmental Psychology, 93*, 102198. https://doi.org/10.1016/j.jenvp.2023.102198

14. Chalmin-Pui, L. S., Griffiths, A., Roe, J., Heaton, T., & Cameron, R. (2021). Why garden? Attitudes and the perceived health benefits of home gardening. *Cities, 112*, 103118. https://doi.org/10.1016/j.cities.2021.103118

15. Lee, M. S., Lee, J., Park, B. J., et al. (2015). Interaction with indoor plants may reduce psychological and physiological stress by suppressing autonomic nervous system activity in young adults: A

randomized crossover study. *Journal of Physiological Anthropology, 34*, 21. https://doi.org/10.1186/s40101-015-0060-8

16. Lu, S., Liu, J., Xu, M., & Xu, F. (2023). Horticultural therapy for stress reduction: A systematic review and meta-analysis. *Frontiers in Psychology, 14*, 1086121. https://doi.org/10.3389/fpsyg.2023.1086121

17. Compitus, K., & Bierbower, S. M. (2024). Cow cuddling: Cognitive considerations in bovine-assisted therapy. *Human-Animal Interactions.* https://doi.org/10.1079/hai.2024.0016

18. Chadwick, Z., Edmondson, A., & McDonald, S. (2022). Engaging with animal-assisted interventions (AAIs): Exploring the experiences of young people with ASD/ADHD diagnoses. *Support for Learning, 37*(1), 44-61. https://doi.org/10.1111/1467-9604.12394

19. McEwan, K., Giles, D., Clarke, F. J., Kotera, Y., Evans, G., Terebenina, O., ... & Weil, D. (2021). A pragmatic controlled trial of forest bathing compared with compassionate mind training in the UK: Impacts on self-reported wellbeing and heart rate variability. *Sustainability, 13*(3), 1380. https://doi.org/10.3390/su13031380

20. Siah, C. J. R., Goh, Y. S., Lee, J., Poon, S. N., Ow Yong, J. Q. Y., & Tam, W. S. W. (2023). The effects of forest bathing on psychological well-being: A systematic review and meta-analysis. *International Journal of Mental Health Nursing, 32*(4), 1038-1054. https://doi.org/10.1111/inm.13131

21. Vainio, K., Korrensalo, A., Takala, T., Räsänen, A., Lummaa, K., & Tuittila, E. S. (2024). Do you have a tree friend? Human–tree relationships in

Finland. *People and Nature, 6*(2), 646-659. https://doi.org/10.1002/pan3.10593

22. Camic, P. M. (2008). Playing in the mud: Health psychology, the arts and creative approaches to health care. *Journal of Health Psychology, 13*(2), 287-298. https://doi.org/10.1177/1359105307086698

23. Lahart, I., Darcy, P., Gidlow, C., & Calogiuri, G. (2019). The effects of green exercise on physical and mental well-being: A systematic review. *International Journal of Environmental Research and Public Health, 16*(8), 1352. https://doi.org/10.3390/ijerph16081352

24. Passmore, H. A., & Krause, A. N. (2023). The beyond-human natural world: Providing meaning and making meaning. *International Journal of Environmental Research and Public Health, 20*(12), 6170. https://doi.org/10.3390/ijerph20126170

25. Howell, A. J., Passmore, H. A., & Buro, K. (2013). Meaning in nature: Meaning in life as a mediator of the relationship between nature connectedness and well-being. *Journal of Happiness Studies, 14*, 1681-1696. https://doi.org/10.1007/s10902-012-9403-x

26. Lackey, N. Q., Tysor, D. A., McNay, G. D., Joyner, L., Baker, K. H., & Hodge, C. (2019). Mental health benefits of nature-based recreation: A systematic review. *Annals of Leisure Research, 24*(3), 379-393. https://doi.org/10.1080/11745398.2019.1655459

27. Shanahan, D. F., Astell-Burt, T., Barber, E. A., Brymer, E., Cox, D. T., Dean, J., ... & Gaston, K. J. (2019). Nature-based interventions for improving health and well-being: The purpose, the people and the outcomes. *Sports, 7*(6), 141. https://doi.org/10.3390/sports7060141

28. Choi, H., Hahm, S. C., Jeon, Y. H., Han, J. W., Kim, S. Y., & Woo, J. M. (2021). The effects of mindfulness-based mandala colouring, made in nature, on chronic widespread musculoskeletal pain: Randomized trial. *Healthcare, 9*(6), 642. https://doi.org/10.3390/healthcare9060642

29. Richardson, M., Passmore, H. A., Barbett, L., Lumber, R., Thomas, R., & Hunt, A. (2020). The green care code: How nature connectedness and simple activities help explain pro-nature conservation behaviours. *People and Nature, 2*(3), 821-839. https://doi.org/10.1002/pan3.10117

30. Baker, K., Chioran, B., & Marks, E. (2024). "Eco-caring together" pro-ecological group-based community interventions and mental well-being: A systematic scoping review. *Frontiers in Psychology, 15*, 1288791. https://doi.org/10.3389/fpsyg.2024.1288791

31. Martin, L., White, M. P., Hunt, A., Richardson, M., Pahl, S., & Burt, J. (2020). Nature contact, nature connectedness and associations with health, well-being, and pro-environmental behaviours. *Journal of Environmental Psychology, 68*, 101389. http://dx.doi.org/10.1016/j.jenvp.2020.101389

Section 3: Spirituality-based Interventions

1. Ravishankar, S. S. (2022). *Patanjali Yoga Sutras*. Sri Sri Publications Trust.

2. Ravishankar, S. S. (2019). *An intimate note to the sincere seeker*. Aslan Business Solutions.

3. De Manincor, M., Bensoussan, A., Smith, C. A., Barr, K., Schweickle, M., Donoghoe, L. L., & Fahey, P. (2016). Individualized yoga for reducing depression

and anxiety and improving well-being: A randomized controlled trial. *Depression and Anxiety, 33*(9), 816-828. https://doi.org/10.1002/da.22502

4. Sahni, P. S., Singh, K., Sharma, N., & Garg, R. (2021). Yoga an effective strategy for self-management of stress-related problems and well-being during COVID-19 lockdown: A cross-sectional study. *PLOS One, 16*(2), e0245214. https://doi.org/10.1371/journal.pone.0245214

5. Chhajer, R., & Dagar, C. (2024). Examining the impact of a restorative breath-based intervention "Sudarshan Kriya Yoga" at work: A field experiment. *Frontiers in Psychology, 15*, 1327119. https://doi.org/10.3389/fpsyg.2024.1327119

6. Tripathy, M., & Sahu, B. (2019). Immediate effect of Nadi Shodhana pranayama on blood glucose, heart rate and blood pressure. *Journal of American Science, 15*(5), 65-70. http://dx.doi.org/10.7537/marsjas150519.09

7. Peckham, S. B., Ionson, E., Nassim, M., Ojha, K., Palaniyappan, L., Gati, J., & Vasudev, A. (2019). Sahaj Samadhi meditation vs a health enhancement program in improving late-life depression severity and executive function: Study protocol for a two-site, randomized controlled trial. *Trials, 20*, 1-16. https://doi.org/10.1186/s13063-019-3682-z

8. Lemay, V., Hoolahan, J., & Buchanan, A. (2019). Impact of a yoga and meditation intervention on students' stress and anxiety levels. *American Journal of Pharmaceutical Education, 83*(5), 7001. https://doi.org/10.5688/ajpe7001

9. Sylapan, B. S., Nair, A. K., Jayanna, K., Mallipeddi, S., Sathyanarayana, S., & Kutty, B. M. (2020).

Meditation, well-being and cognition in heartfulness meditators–A pilot study. *Consciousness and Cognition, 86,* 103032. https://doi.org/10.1016/j.concog.2020.103032

10. Moszeik, E. N., von Oertzen, T., & Renner, K. H. (2022). Effectiveness of a short Yoga Nidra meditation on stress, sleep, and well-being in a large and diverse sample. *Current Psychology, 41,* 5272-5286. https://doi.org/10.1007/s12144-020-01042-2

11. Nickolas, M., Hayes, A., Hughes, P., Hammer, D., Clarke, A., Pargament, K., & Doehring, C. (2009). Perceiving sacredness in life: Correlates and predictors. *Archive for the Psychology of Religion, 31*(1), 55-73. https://doi.org/10.1163/157361209X371492

12. Goldstein, E. D. (2007). Sacred moments: Implications on well-being and stress. *Journal of Clinical Psychology, 63*(10), 1001-1019. https://doi.org/10.1002/jclp.20402

13. Brown, K. M., Hoye, R., & Nicholson, M. (2012). Self-esteem, self-efficacy, and social connectedness as mediators of the relationship between volunteering and well-being. *Journal of Social Service Research, 38*(4), 468-483. https://doi.org/10.1080/01488376.2012.687706

14. Jiang, D., Warner, L. M., Chong, A. M. L., Li, T., Wolff, J. K., & Chou, K. L. (2021). Benefits of volunteering on psychological well-being in older adulthood: Evidence from a randomized controlled trial. *Aging & Mental Health, 25*(4), 641-649. https://doi.org/10.1080/13607863.2020.1711862

15. Wang, Y., & Wu, R. (2022). The effect of fasting on human metabolism and psychological

health. *Disease Markers, 2022*(1), 5653739. https://doi.org/10.1155/2022/5653739

16. Min, S., Masanovic, B., Bu, T., Matic, R. M., Vasiljevic, I., Vukotic, M., & Popovic, S. (2021). The association between regular physical exercise, sleep patterns, fasting, and autophagy for healthy longevity and well-being: A narrative review. *Frontiers in Psychology, 12*, 803421. https://doi.org/10.3389/fpsyg.2021.803421

17. Palgi, Y., Segel-Karpas, D., Ost Mor, S., Hoffman, Y., Shrira, A., & Bodner, E. (2021). Positive solitude scale: Theoretical background, development and validation. *Journal of Happiness Studies*, 1-28. https://doi.org/10.1007/s10902-021-00367-4

18. Nguyen, T. T., Ryan, R. M., & Deci, E. L. (2018). Solitude as an approach to affective self-regulation. *Personality and Social Psychology Bulletin, 44*(1), 92-106. https://doi.org/10.1177/0146167217733073

19. Kang, J., Martinez, C. M. J., & Johnson, C. (2021). Minimalism as a sustainable lifestyle: Its behavioral representations and contributions to emotional well-being. *Sustainable Production and Consumption, 27*, 802-813. https://doi.org/10.1016/j.spc.2021.02.001

20. Ran, R. (2024). Ancient wisdom in the modern world: Loving-kindness and compassion meditations for psychological well-being. *Clinical Psychology: Science and Practice, 31*(1), 36–38. https://doi.org/10.1037/cps0000184

21. Perry, G., Polito, V., Sankaran, N., & Thompson, W. F. (2022). How chanting relates to cognitive function, altered states and quality of life. *Brain Sciences, 12*(11), 1456. https://doi.org/10.3390/brainsci12111456

22. Toussaint, L., & Webb, J. R. (2005). Theoretical and empirical connections between forgiveness,

mental health, and well-being. In *Handbook of Forgiveness* (pp. 349-362).

23. Harris, A. H., Luskin, F., Norman, S. B., Standard, S., Bruning, J., Evans, S., & Thoresen, C. E. (2006). Effects of a group forgiveness intervention on forgiveness, perceived stress, and trait-anger. *Journal of Clinical Psychology, 62*(6), 715-733. https://doi.org/10.1002/jclp.20264

24. Fernández-Campos, S., Roca, P., & Yaden, M. B. (2021). The impermanence awareness and acceptance scale. *Mindfulness, 12,* 1542–1554. https://doi.org/10.1007/s12671-021-01623-7

25. Perry, G., Polito, V., Sankaran, N., & Thompson, W. F. (2022). How chanting relates to cognitive function, altered states, and quality of life. *Brain Sciences, 12*(11), 1456. https://doi.org/10.3390/brainsci12111456

26. Astin, A. W., & Keen, J. P. (2006). Equanimity and spirituality. *Religion and Education, 33*(2), 39-46. http://dx.doi.org/10.1080/15507394.2006.10012375

27. Smith, W. L., & Zhang, P. (2011). A spiritual getaway: The motivations, experiences, and benefits of a silent retreat. In *Research in the Social Scientific Study of Religion* (Vol. 22, pp. 1-24). Brill. https://doi.org/10.1163/ej.9789004207271.i-360.7

28. Aulet, S. (2024). The transformational potential of visiting sacred sites. In *Religious Tourism and Globalization: The Search for Identity and Transformative Experience* (pp. 57-70). CABI. https://doi.org/10.1079/9781800623675.0005

29. Perriam, G. (2015). Sacred spaces, healing places: Therapeutic landscapes of spiritual

significance. *Journal of Medical Humanities, 36*, 19-33. https://doi.org/10.1007/s10912-014-9318-0

30. Felver, J. C., Jones, R., Killam, M. A., et al. (2017). Contemplative intervention reduces physical interventions for children in residential psychiatric treatment. *Prevention Science, 18*, 164–173. https://doi.org/10.1007/s11121-016-0720-x

Section 4: Art-based Interventions

1. Csikszentmihalyi, M. (2020). *Finding flow: The psychology of engagement with everyday life.* Hachette UK.

2. Nakamura, J., & Csikszentmihalyi, M. (2002). The concept of flow. In *Handbook of positive psychology* (pp. 89-105). Oxford University Press. https://psycnet.apa.org/record/2002-02382-007

3. Dunphy, K., Mullane, S., & Jacobsson, M. (2014). The effectiveness of expressive arts therapies: A review of the literature. *Psychotherapy and Counselling Journal of Australia, 2*(1). https://doi.org/10.59158/001c.71004

4. Jenabi, E., Bashirian, S., Ayubi, E., Rafiee, M., & Bashirian, M. (2023). The effect of the art therapy interventions on depression symptoms among older adults: A meta-analysis of controlled clinical trials. *Journal of Geriatric Psychiatry and Neurology, 36*(3), 185-192. https://doi.org/10.1177/08919887221130264

5. Joschko, R., Klatte, C., Grabowska, W. A., Roll, S., Berghöfer, A., & Willich, S. N. (2024). Active visual art therapy and health outcomes: A systematic review and meta-analysis. *JAMA Network*

Open, 7(9), e2428709. https://doi.org/10.1001/jamanetworkopen.2024.28709

6. Hinz, L. D. (2019). *Expressive therapies continuum: A framework for using art in therapy*. Routledge. https://doi.org/10.4324/9780429299339

7. Gross, J. J. (1998). The emerging field of emotion regulation: An integrative review. *Review of General Psychology, 2*(3), 271–299. https://doi.org/10.1037/1089-2680.2.3.271

8. Kumar, V., Pavitra, K. S., & Bhattacharya, R. (2024). Creative pursuits for mental health and well-being. *Indian Journal of Psychiatry, 66*(Suppl 2), S283-S303. https://pubmed.ncbi.nlm.nih.gov/38445283/

9. Garnefski, N., van den Kommer, T., Kraaij, V., Teerds, J., Legerstee, J., & Onstein, E. (2002). The relationship between cognitive emotion regulation strategies and emotional problems: Comparison between a clinical and a non-clinical sample. *European Journal of Personality, 16*(5), 403-420. https://psycnet.apa.org/doi/10.1002/per.458

10. Song, H., Chan, J. S., & Ryan, C. (2024). Differences and similarities in the use of nine emotion regulation strategies in Western and East-Asian cultures: Systematic review and meta-analysis. *Journal of Cross-Cultural Psychology*, 00220221241285006. http://dx.doi.org/10.1177/00220221241285006

11. Williams, E., Dingle, G. A., Jetten, J., & Rowan, C. (2019). Identification with arts-based groups improves mental well-being in adults with chronic mental health conditions. *Journal of Applied Social Psychology, 49*(1), 15-26. https://doi.org/10.1111/jasp.12561

12. Caló, F., Steiner, A., Millar, S., & Teasdale, S. (2020). The impact of a community-based music intervention on the health and well-being of young people: A realist evaluation. *Health & Social Care in the Community, 28*(3), 988-997. https://doi.org/10.1111/hsc.12931

13. Kramer, Z., Pellegrini, V., Kramer, G., et al. (2023). Effects of insight dialogue retreats on mindfulness, self-compassion, and psychological well-being. *Mindfulness, 14*, 746–756. https://doi.org/10.1007/s12671-022-02045-9

14. Hadley, R., Eastwood-Gray, O., Kiddier, M., Rose, D., & Ponzo, S. (2020). "Dance like nobody's watching": Exploring the role of dance-based interventions in perceived well-being and bodily awareness in people with Parkinson's. *Frontiers in Psychology, 11*, 531567. https://doi.org/10.3389/fpsyg.2020.531567

15. Ajayi Olayemi, T., & Omisakin, F. W. T. (2024). Assessing the feasibility and effectiveness of origami as a viable tool for health enhancements in a post-pandemic era. *European Journal of Modern Medicine and Practice, 4*(4), 296–303. https://www.inovatus.es/index.php/ejmmp/article/view/3076

16. Mosko, J. E., & Delach, M. J. (2021). Cooking, creativity, and well-being: An integration of quantitative and qualitative methods. *The Journal of Creative Behavior, 55*(2), 348-361. https://doi.org/10.1002/jocb.459

17. Sonker, S., Sharma, V., & Mishra, S. (2024). Impact of art-based therapies on mental health and well-being. *ResearchGate.* https://www.researchgate.net/publication/381265328_Impact_of_Art-Based_Therapies_on_Mental_Health_and_Wellbeing

18. Cox, A., & Brewster, L. (2018). Photo-a-day: A digital photographic practice and its impact on well-being. *Photographies, 11*(1), 113–129. https://doi.org/10.1080/17540763.2017.1399288

19. Pöllänen, S. H., & Weissmann-Hanski, M. K. (2019). Hand-made well-being: Textile crafts as a source of eudaimonic well-being. *Journal of Leisure Research, 51*(3), 348–365. https://doi.org/10.1080/00222216.2019.1688738

20. Brown, A. (2020). Connecting with a place through making a video. *Geography, 105*(1), 26–33. https://doi.org/10.1080/00167487.2020.12094085

21. Chalmin-Pui, L. S., Roe, J., Griffiths, A., Smyth, N., Heaton, T., Clayden, A., & Cameron, R. (2021). "It made me feel brighter in myself": The health and well-being impacts of a residential front garden horticultural intervention. *Landscape and Urban Planning, 205*, 103958. https://doi.org/10.1016/j.landurbplan.2020.103958

22. Crawford, S. A., & Caltabiano, N. J. (2011). Promoting emotional well-being through the use of humour. *The Journal of Positive Psychology, 6*(3), 237–252. https://doi.org/10.1080/17439760.2011.577087

23. Pérez-Sáez, E., Cabrero-Montes, E. M., Llorente-Cano, M., & González-Ingelmo, E. (2020). A pilot study on the impact of a pottery workshop on the well-being of people with dementia. *Dementia, 19*(6), 2056-2072. https://doi.org/10.1177/1471301218814634

24. Jensen, C. M., & Blair, S. E. (1997). Rhyme and reason: The relationship between creative writing and mental well-being. *British Journal of Occupational Therapy, 60*(12), 525-530. https://doi.org/10.1177/030802269706001205

25. Prati, G. (2022). The association between sense of community and support for local farmers' market. *Community Psychology in Global Perspective, 8*(2), 24–36. https://doi.org/10.1285/i24212113v8i2p24

26. De Bloom, J., Nawijn, J., Geurts, S., Kinnunen, U., & Korpela, K. (2017). Holiday travel, staycations, and subjective well-being. *Journal of Sustainable Tourism, 25*(4), 573-588. https://doi.org/10.1080/09669582.2016.1229323

27. Huang, X., Wang, P., & Wu, L. (2024). Well-being through transformation: An integrative framework of transformative tourism experiences and hedonic versus eudaimonic well-being. *Journal of Travel Research, 63*(4), 974-994. https://doi.org/10.1177/00472875231171670

Please scan the QR code for the link to resources.

Acknowledgments

This journey would not have been possible without the support, guidance, and love of many remarkable individuals and communities.

Thank you, Juhi Goyal, for assisting me throughout this book writing project. Your support and dedication have been invaluable.

To Shrea Porwal, the brilliant illustrator, your talent is a true gift, and I am grateful for your partnership.

I would like to acknowledge academic researchers and practitioners in the field of mental health and well-being whose insights have been instrumental in shaping these interventions.

To Gurudev Sri Sri Ravi Shankar, for his boundless spiritual wisdom, SKY breathwork, and meditation practices that have nurtured my soul and guided my path, I offer my deepest gratitude.

A special thanks to the community of artists, whose passion and dedication to their craft have been a constant source of inspiration.

I would like to express my sincere appreciation to IIM Indore, my workplace, for fostering an environment that encourages innovation and exploration.

Lastly, to my beloved family and friends, thank you for your unwavering support, love, and encouragement. You have been my strength throughout this journey, and I am forever grateful for your presence in my life.

Author Bio

Dr. Raina Chhajer is an Assistant Professor of Psychology at the Indian Institute of Management Indore, India. Her research focuses on positive psychology, mental health, nature connectedness, yoga, breathwork, and meditation. Her work has been published in esteemed international peer-reviewed journals including *Mindfulness, BMC Public Health, Frontiers in Psychology, Neuroscience Insights*, and *Frontiers in Public Health*.

Dr. Chhajer brings an interdisciplinary approach to teaching, offering innovative courses such as *'Thriving at Work,' 'The Art and Science of Yoga,'* and *'Nature and Well-Being.'* She has also designed and led leadership development programs for industry executives, with impactful trainings like *'Leading with Purpose,' 'Leading for Excellence at Work,'* and *'Mindfulness-Based Leadership.'*

A certified forest therapy guide by the Association of Forest and Nature Therapy (ANFT), USA, Dr. Chhajer integrates nature-based practices into her work, reflecting her deep interest in nature connectedness. Additionally, she is a certified yoga instructor through the Sri Sri School of Yoga and actively conducts research on the impact of yoga on mental health and well-being.

Beyond academia, Dr. Chhajer is also committed to social causes, supporting girl child education and advocating for environmental conservation. She volunteers with Sri Sri Gyan Mandir Parola, a school dedicated to providing free education to tribal girls in Rajasthan, and with Embrace Nature Foundation, which promotes environmental education and tree plantation.

Through her combined roles as an academic, researcher, and practitioner, Dr. Chhajer remains dedicated to promoting mental health and well-being in both academic and professional settings.

LinkedIn: linkedin.com/in/rainachhajer
Instagram: @bewell_with_raina

Please scan the QR code to follow me on Instagram.